success @ life

NEWMARKET PRESS

New York

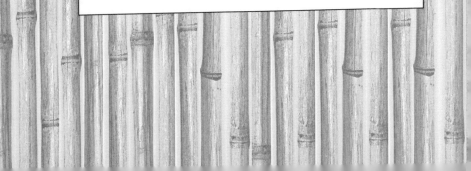

success@life

A Zentrepreneur's Guide

How to Catch and Live Your Dream

RON RUBIN AND STUART AVERY GOLD

MINISTERS OF

The REPUBLIC of TEA

Interior graphics by Image Studio Ltd.

Calligraphy by Alan Atkinson, Ph.D.

FIRST EDITION
2 3 4 5 6 7 8 9 10

Library of Congress Cataloging-in-Publication Data

Rubin, Ron.
    Success @ life : how to catch and live your dream : a Zentrepreneur's guide / by Ron Rubin and Stuart Avery Gold.--1st ed.
        p. cm.
    Includes bibliographical references.
    ISBN 1-55704-476-7 (alk. paper)
    1. Success—Psychological aspects. I. Title: Success at life.
II. Rubin, Ron. III. Gold, Stuart Avery. IV. Title.
BF637.S8 R78 2001
158--dc211
                                                    2001030203
                                                    CIP

QUANTITY PURCHASES
Companies, professional groups, clubs, and other organizations may qualify for special terms when ordering quantities of this title. For information, write Special Sales, Newmarket Press, 18 East 48th Street, New York, NY 10017, call (212) 832-3575, fax (212) 832-3629, or e-mail mail@newmarketpress.com

website www.newmarketpress.com

Manufactured in the United States of America.
At the authors' request, this book has been printed on acid-free paper.

Go confidently in the direction of your dreams.

Live the life you imagined.

—Henry David Thoreau

Contents

The REPUBLIC of TEA

Dear Fellow Zentrepreneurs,

From travels afar, the Minister of Tea and I send you sip by sip regards from our outpost nested on the steep slopes overlooking the verdant tea gardens near Hangzhou, the ancient capital of Song dynasty China. Soon the sun will decide to rise, cutting the mist, and we will once again gleefully begin our journey of many cups, searching and sampling exquisite rare teas. The same rare teas that Mao Tse-tung drank with Richard Nixon not too far down the road on that East meets West historic day. With tomorrow's first light, we will make the breathtaking exotic trek to the cloud-shrouded mountainsides of Yunnan, the birthplace of tea, where wild tea trees still grow, the most ancient and revered of them being over seventeen hundred years old.

For us this is a wondrous journey outside space and time, where heaven comes down to earth and teaches us once more that the true path to happiness begins with who we are. For us, tea has been a nurturing guide that continues to inspire us to dream and do. We humbly offer up ourselves as proof to those who are confused about their place in the world and their direction in it. Know that we wake excitedly each day, to live the lives that we have always imagined, no longer fantasizing adventure in faraway places, our dreams have become the catalyst for delivering us there. Doing what you want to do, being what you want to be, no person who feels as we could hide from such harmony and happiness.

This book is about dreaming and doing, an opportunity to present a path or power that will allow you to create for yourself a success @ life that reflects who you truly are. It's about being guided by an inner-wind that can transport you to a place and time where your dreams can and will come true. Ultimately it is about the joy-filled destiny you can and must shape for yourself by embracing dreaming and being. That said, it pleases us to invite you to let go of the nightmarish unreality of the reality that has hold of you and give yourself over to the splendor of the dream waiting to have you. It is as simple and as exciting as that.

Yours in the Spirit of Change,

Travel

The Minister of Travel

HUN DUN

BEFORE
THE
BEGINNING

The flavor of Zen and

the flavor of tea is the same.

—Japanese Proverb

The decision to write this book was made over a cup of tea.

No biggie.

Truth to tell, a lot of the decisions that we make are over a cup of a tea. The reality of the reason being that we spend many hours a day and more running a neat little California company called—suitably enough—The Republic of Tea.

Now maybe you have heard of it; The Republic of Tea is a progressive and socially conscious business recognized for being the leading purveyor of only the most exquisite teas and herbs in the world. The awards for our products and innovative and artful packaging are legend in the industry.

Or perhaps you have seen it. We sell more than one hundred varieties of teas, herbs, healthy chai tea lattes, bottled iced teas, tea jams, tea cookies, the pots, the cups and a ton of other tea-related products, in more than twenty thousand gourmet and specialty food retailers, restaurants and cafes throughout the country. Plus, there is a beautiful exclusive catalogue and a Web site (of course!) that we happily invite you to visit.

But probably this all matters not, since many of you dear readers are more than likely hooked on a somewhat darker brew consisting of the oily opiate of the roasted bean. So let me pause for a quick moment to point out the reason for the above excursion into such blatant commercial plugging.

Two reasons actually.

First, and please believe it, the most important reason is this: growing the business of The Republic of Tea is a powerful passion with us. Every day we go to work feeling a thousand years younger, because we do what we love and love what we do. The challenges, opportunities and excitement of finding new ways to market civilization's oldest beverage and of building a brand to thrive over the long run have inspired and changed our lives in many a grand way.

The second reason?

The other book.

A book that we had absolutely nothing whatsoever to do with. But, nevertheless, a book that has only everything to do with why this written endeavor exists. Authored by Mel Ziegler, Patricia Ziegler and Bill Rosenzweig, and published by Currency Doubleday, *Fortune Magazine* said of it: "Like no other book, it conveys with charm and insight how business builders think as they struggle to realize their dreams." The title of this other book:

The Republic of Tea.

And if you were to research the reviews, you would find that there were many and that they were all golden.

So much deservedly so, that the book has become required reading for college courses and business classes around the country—a how-to story of vision, risk and success to help guide anyone who dares to dream.

But again, placing all credit at the doorstep where it is due, once more we want to stress that we had absolutely nothing whatsoever to do with the existence, substance or success of that book.

Zilch. Zippo. Nada.

Still, here is as good as place as any to thank Mel, Patricia and Bill for their creation and with full hearts wish them continued joy.

Because this book in some ways is primarily what their book was primarily about—how to sip from cups filled to the brim with your hearts hopes and desires. That, however, is where similarities between the two books end. The providential difference being: The book they wrote, *The Republic of Tea,* was a book the authors wanted to write. The book *Success @ Life* is a book we had to write.

No choice.

Not since in this world there are only twenty-four hours in a day. And the school week begins on Monday and wraps on Friday. And you can add this:

It is becoming more and more difficult to show up for class.

Let me briefly explain.

As owner of The Republic of Tea, it's amazing how many invitations Ron receives and gladly accepts from universities across the country to come guest lecture and spiel his practical and entertaining insights and zentrepreneurial wisdom to can-do students hungry to absorb the essence of what it takes to succeed, to live the lives they imagine and dream of. And since this book is not totally without ego, please know that he is flattered by their requests, touched by their heat, buoyed by their attention, and greatly moved by their talent, determination and enthusiasm. Magic moments. And I only mention this because if only there were more time in the day or more days in the week, this is something he/we would really like to be able to do more often—give of ourselves fully to the inexhaustible creators of tomorrow.

But we can't.

Simply put, the demands on our time have become increasingly greater as we try to stay compassed to the course of our own dream—to unleash on the world what we have come to realize as The Art of Tea. So when many a kind invitation comes our way to address a bunch of brightners with a wish to succeed and we find we must return it with regret, because of a trip to the misty green tea gardens of China, we are dejected. When another cordial request must be turned away because of a committed trek through the famed tea provinces of India or the mountains of Japan, we are despaired. Greatly. Because we are true believers in the axiom that speaks to the human spirit and says, that we make a living by what we get, but we make a life by what we give.

And so it goes. More and more frequently we find ourselves turning down an experience that we hold in high regard, and we are frustrated. Because do we want to say yes, yes, yes to all of these wonderful solicitations? You betcha. God knows we want to come talk, listen and answer questions with these students for an hour, and help illuminate their paths as others have crucially and gloriously held a light to ours. We want to be there to urge them to dream the biggest dreams and to clue them into the fact that the world is open to talent, and the only limitations on their lives are the ones they put on themselves. We want so much to embolden them to know that they are all so goddamn gifted and that each of them possesses the ability to shine—to become jade amongst the stones. We want to be able to voice all this and very much more. But remember again, the school week begins on Monday and wraps on Friday and on each of those days and on the frenetic ones in between, what precious time there is, is calendared to carry the weight of our own dream and so, alas, like we said:

No choice.

Except to write this book.

And share the dream.

But to better prepare you for the pilgrimage of pages that lie ahead, it is important that we register here one or two touchstones for the reader, a little perspective that will allow us to address the empowering force within you, awaiting release. As Ministers of The Republic of Tea, our not-so-covert mission is to carry out a Tea Revolution. Our free and open immigration policies welcome all who wish to flee the tyranny of coffee crazed lives and escape the frazzled fast-paced race-to-stay-in-one-place existence that it fuels. In our tiny land, we have come to learn that coffee is about speeding up and losing sight, while tea is about slowing down and taking a look. Because tea is not just a beverage, it is a consciousness-altering substance that allows for a way of getting in touch with and taking pleasure from the beauty and the wonder that life has to offer.

Slow down. Be grateful. Bow to the distinctiveness that is you: your mind, your body, your spirit and your splendor. In The Republic of Tea we embody the words of Lao-Tzu who said, "Knowing others is wisdom, knowing yourself is Enlightenment." Our desire is that through the flawless pearl of what we have come to define as TeaMind, people will learn to locate the source of their innate *Self*, discovering the satisfaction and the serenity of their natural and true paths. We are humbled to report that by all accounts our collective efforts and passionate energy seem to be meeting with success. The pin-striped brigade that tabulates whatever it is they tabulate say that our brand is flourishing—a direct result of millions of TeaMinded citizens defecting to our state. Drawn by the youth of the water and the gift of the leaf, they seek asylum in our fanciful Republic. Our purpose has always been to enrich people's lives through the experience of fine teas and the sip by sip way of life—a life of health, balance and well-being. Our way is to educate, inspire and communicate the quality, benefits, values and lifestyle of The Republic of Tea, by presenting a metaphor for a life that is attentive and happy. We believe that if a simple cup of tea can cause one to slow down and pay attention, if with a single sip, the cloud of a busy mind is made to pass and people are able to, however briefly, transcend from the realm of form into the formless realm—and thus gain a fuller realization and appreciation of their own true nature, talents, hopes and dreams, then we say nothing can be more inspiring.

The point being: The Republic of Tea has been for us, still, always, a special way of life, an odyssey that sets an example of what a twenty-first century entrepreneur—a *Zentrepreneur*—is all about. If you are seeking a liberating career change that expresses and fulfills your talents, passions and dreams, if you are an undergrad, an MBA, or maybe someone who never went to college but possesses a can-do attitude, and you are unfamiliar with the term *Zentrepreneur*, now is the time to license yourself and drive it home into a clearing in your cranium. Both hands on the wheel, park it properly for easy access. At your darkest hour, it is the term that will barrel you toward daylight, giving you the clarity and power that will help you become what you always dreamed of, but never thought you could be:

A Master of your own destiny.

Recently, Ron and I had the opportunity to step beyond the busyness of daily attachments and share some time and spirit with an editor of a prominent national magazine. She came to us preparing an article on tea. We welcomed her by preparing a pot of tea. It wasn't too long before our visitor from back east abandoned the entanglements of her world and quickly fell under the fragrant clouds and tranquil spell of a cup of full-leaf Jasmine Pearls, a rare tea that seldom makes its way to western cups. Now, we are always honored when we are able to bring tea to people—or people to tea—and so it was that we were honored twice that day. First by the oneness that sharing a cup of tea creates between host and guest, and then once again by the sincere heart and spirit of her many questions, one of which was, and these were her words: "What is a Zentrepreneur?"

Simple.

It wasn't the first time we had been asked that question. But it was the first time that we were more than delighted to answer, you see, because coincidentally on this occasion, we had the added kicker of using props. Which we promptly did. Ron began by pouring the steamy tea from the teapot into our visitor's cup, carefully paying attention, skillfully filling it up to the very brim until the cup overflowed and no more tea would go in. Our visitor watched, stunned indeed. "Like the cup, you are full of your own opinions and expectations," Ron explained, paraphrasing a Japanese master. "How can we tell you what a Zentrepreneur is unless you first empty your cup?"

Looking back now, nice explanation, that. Because in the interest of accuracy, that is what a Zentrepreneur is: someone who risks letting go of preconceived notions in order to deepen their knowledge of self—and beyond. Someone who endeavors to study and practice, to live a life where the creative spark, the inner illumination of spirit, talent and uniqueness, is put into motion, fostering growth that not only enriches one's own life, but the lives of others as well. But more than that, a Zentrepreneur is someone who has made his or her own life noble and rich beyond counting by simply *living a dream defined*. While an entrepreneur creates a business, a Zentrepreneur creates a business and a life.

And that is what the pulse of this book is about. Why we had to bring it to life: to give back in some way the roughbone formula, the unearthed ideas, deepened beliefs, practical philosophies, and shhhh. . . the secrets we have learned along the radiant journey to living our own dreams.

So without regard for our personal sanity we have decided to collaborate on this book. Using our gathered energies as battle-beaten Zentrepreneurs—Ron, with his unique experience of building successful businesses, and me with my experience and ability to create their flourish—we made the decision to spill blood together and with fingers very much crossed, go to war with empty pages.

And now you know.

—*Stuart Avery Gold*

REQING

Chapter One
LIVE YOUR PASSION

LIFE IS BUT A DREAM

Look within—

The secret is inside you.

—Hui-neng

Heavy.

That's what they said when they would lift the black, travel-worn salesman's sample case.

Heavy to carry and full of weight—with a frayed hanging-on-to-what-was-left handle, corners that twenty-something years of road trotting, give or take, had tattered. You looked at it and knew that it had decades ago seen better days and thought, why tote such a thing? What with all the wonders Samsonite has brought to the world: telescopic handles, retractable wheels, Velcro this and Velcro that. Even a grunt MBA could appreciate that there were easier ways to journey through airports and taxi around than to lug such a torment and eyesore.

In fact, why travel with such a dread at all?

That's what colleagues and associates wondered. Certainly something wafer thin and glorious from Coach or Cartier would be more fitting for my friend Ron, whose success and business acumen had been validated and lauded. Absolutely the price for such things had not for a long time now been an issue. The point being, this was an anomaly that only a few could figure out, and even fewer could understand. In other words, what's up with the shit dinosaur sample case?

The answer was simple.

Inside the hefty beat-up hopelessly dated black case were, please believe me, shhhh . . .

Secrets.

Hiking back through the years.

Spring. Ron's first day out of college. First real job. Salesman. Wholesale liquor salesman to be exact. Son of the owner to be more exact.

Not an easy life.

I don't think most people realize—and why should they?—the amount of demeaning crap you have to take when you want to join the family business. If you become a doctor, an accountant or a stockbroker, you walk into work every day chest out, your head high, no problem. But want to follow your passion and become part of the life that always accompanied your father home, from the first morning you show up the look on the faces of your fellow employees will tell of a terrible fate that will soon be told. At first you're welcomed with open arms. Then you're flattered, and then yadda, yadda, you're flattered some more.

And why shouldn't you be, sure you're the owner's son, but after all, you are immaculately bright and wondrously talented and hard working and energetic and of course life at that moment was so on an upswing. What a wonderful feeling it is to think this is how work will be—every day the sunrise bringing acceptance and favor.

Wrong.

It was only twenty-three minutes into the first hour of the first morning on the first day when the heavy crash of reality came thundering down on Ron.

Now the following might not seem like it's worth even a paragraph, but please follow me—it is—as you will hopefully see in the pages and chapters to come.

A brief narrative about the wholesale liquor business—a tremendous behemoth of a business, even more so now than in years past when Ron started out. Today, those who pitch the Chardonnays, Cabernets, and Merlots, along with assorted spirits and ales to our eateries, hotels and corner package stores, are huuuuge monstrous gajillion-dollar companies, with a highly educated and well-trained sales force whose numbers are legion.

Not so back then.

Back then the business was the province of tenacious small businessmen with no formal education, but who understood the politics and workings of their towns. They worked it street-by-street, corner-by-corner to sell and service every account possible. These sales were made by a handful of wing-tipped whiskey salesmen who navigated their way in ashtray-filled Oldsmobiles, their pockets weighed with change to report in (no cell phones, pagers or office e-mail in those prehistoric times). And though their work took them from one continental cuisine establishment to the next, meals were sandwiches and potato chips, nothing that required utensils, because who had time to sit down when every commission was so hair-pullingly earned? Every day was like the day before. You called on an account, shmoozed, made the sale, took the order and got the hell out. Seldom did a day end at five. Never did anybody think it would. Hard work for those who had been at it for a while. Shit work for those who wanted at it.

In other words, be careful what you wish for.

Now maybe if they *wanted* someone whose verve and vim could show them some real sales technique that wasn't from the previous century—maybe they would have listened to Ron's every suggestion. And maybe if a college degree and the kind of whizbang hotshot intensity that a spirited youth can bring to the party were something they were scouting for, they would have taken full advantage of Ron and gone with him all the way.

But only maybe.

Understand, when you're a racehorse full of oats, you're ready to run, and when you bolt the gate, watch out because there isn't a single soul who wouldn't be startled at how fast you can pull away and bring it home. But do you want to know the truth?

Getting started was like glue.

Ron could not, repeat, could *not* believe it. He did not see how such a thing was possible. Because, and here's the thing, along with a repertoire that included a sat and studied for college sheepskin, there was—and now get ready for it, here it comes—a full year of turning hours upside down at U. C. Davis fiercely mastering viticulture and enology.

Ho-hum, right?

Agreed. A yawn subject of no interest for most, but if you wanted to gain knowledge and insight of all that can be learned about the art of the grape and the vintage and value of port, and if it was your passion to know what makes a '61 Lafite one of the great wines of our lifetime, then this was a classroom you were every green day glad to enter. A great personal experience at the time, which was so remarkable, because—and now commit this to memory, it's v e e r r y important:

Ready?

Once you find a passionate interest, it hits you, permeates your mind. Truly. It creates a continuous array of bright spots, an elation and excitement that can absolutely, positively, one hundred percent, provide you with the most important tool you will need to achieve success. Drum-roll, please (for effect only, but if it helps to drum this into your noodle, all the better):

Discovering your passion will ignite the fire and fan the flames of your dreams and desires. Living your passion will put the world on notice that you are different. Different because your life is more purposeful, fulfilling, joyous and exciting. Passion provides you with the best possible odds to successfully catch and live your dream.

Again, file this away:

Passion breeds excitement, excitement breeds success.

But more about this in a sec.

Briefly now, the lesson that is equally important to remember here is simply this: If you carefully prepare, come to the table pumped with talent and skills that are second to none, but more than that, if you bring along with you a gourmand discipline with all the learnings that your bean can hold, but even much *more* than that, if you possess the chutzpah it takes to walk barefoot over broken glass, you know what?

Forget it, it all means nothing.

Why?

Easy answer.

In business, to every new face you meet, and every handshake you extend, you are one thing and one thing only—you are cookie-cutter conveyor-belt standard. There is, believe it, nothing you can do or show new under their sun, until you prove otherwise.

Quick story:

Two editors at the *New York Times* are sitting around beating a dead horse, discussing yet another idea about yet another feature story on the new millennium. One asked the other who he thought was the most significant, influential human being living today: Whose reach impacts us all one way or another on a daily basis?

"The Pope?"

Not the Pope.

Pause. "The President?"

Nope. It wasn't the President.

Again a pause. Mind totally blank, but working. "Can't be Greenspan at the Fed?"

He was right. It wasn't.

Stymied. One eye closed sighted in thought. Then in

a snap, his genius breaking through: "Duh, where's my head? Rupert Murdoch. Worldwide media mogul, almost the fourth branch of government. He can set the agenda—control the flow of information."

Murdoch was not even a thought.

Things were getting desperate, the ship starting to tank. Going down fast. And before things started going glug, glug, the other man gave the answer. (It was Bill Gates.)

You could see the gears turning before the first one finally replied, "You claim Bill Gates? Nerdy Bill Gates?" Finally, after a third and final pause, quick head nod. "You're right."

And you know what?

He was, of course, right.

Bill and his software are changing the world every morning we get out of bed, proving that there is no law that says you have to have a college degree to become the richest person in the world.

College?

Bill Gates was a dropout. Bailed from Harvard after his third year to devote himself full boogie to his passion, computer work. At a time when other twenty-year-olds were stuck in a course of contemporary literature, the time saved from college placed our Billy boy in his garage, fiddling with the beginnings of what would make him a phenomenon, the premier player in brain-ware. And it's not the least bit inconceivable, that had Billy stayed in college, perhaps hung around going for a

Ph.D., someone else today would be the holder of the world's greatest fortune, which provides us with another important tidbit for you to commit to your cranium:

All degrees are absolutely essential, but essentially worthless.

Depending.

Depending on what?

Depending on you and what you need to achieve your individual passion and dream.

In other words, if you have a burning desire to study something: go to college.

Likewise, if it is your dream to become a doctor, a lawyer, a pharmacist, a therapist, a teacher or some other career in a specialized field that requires generalized knowledge:

Go to college.

And if your sights are set on holding a lucrative position in banking, business management, architectural design or maybe some sort of precision engineering, well, you get the idea:

Go to college.

And if you rule that it isn't a grievous and damaging error to ignore your heart, putting off your true aspirations and dreams in order to please your family and the educrats who would deter you from following your innermost longings and desires, then I wouldn't give the time of day for your soul, but nevertheless, fine, it's your call, so by all means:

Go to college.

But if you have second thoughts about the importance and/or necessity of a degree to accomplish what is burning inside of you, and if you are willing to work like hell and crank it hard in order to make your dreams a reality and thus become an infinitely happier human, then class, make no mistake, you are staring into the looking glass, facing one of the great truths where you have to decide if the image you're making is the image you see. And as you look into the mirror, ask yourself these nagging questions: *What is it in my heart that I must do or be? Do I have what it takes to summon the courage to be true to myself and follow my imagination and passion?*

Welcome to the Crossroad of Chaos.

A stomach-churning time where it is not remotely unusual to feel frustrated, panicked, confused, miserable, frightened, ridiculed, jacked around and even useless.

And many, maybe most, don't arrive here at an early age. The ultimate challenge of taking charge of your own destiny can happen at any age. Even if you have achieved the reward of a degree, if you find that the path you've taken doesn't work for you, be kind to yourself; pull up anchor and make a move beyond the conventional patterns of wisdom that say you are what your college diploma, friends, family and associates say you are. You simply must not allow anything or anyone to lay a trip on you. The whole point is, in order to pursue your passion and acquire the happiness you absolutely deserve, you must not be afraid to turn your back on the opinions of others or the investment and time spent on a degree.

Howard Schultz wasn't afraid.

He refused to follow what was for him, the unnatural path of his family's well-meaning expectations for his future. After graduating from college, he staggered. Despite the pleading of his parents he drifted from a career in sales, desperately looking for some kind of work that would capture his heart and soul, when a few years later, he too found himself standing at the Crossroad of Chaos—a place where the pressure and ignorance of others kill countless ideas and optimistic plans. But in a very real sense, the bold decision to pursue one's passion has genius, magic and power in it. And as any king salmon knows, it's no piece of cake to go swim upstream. Yet the very fact that they *do it* is proof that helps to illustrate this: Something that is seemingly impossible can be achieved once the *decision* to wake up and succeed is made. And now every day, millions around the world are grateful that Howard Schultz decided to wake up and smell the coffee. His decision at the Crossroad of Chaos was to ignore the voices that would derail him, and, instead, take that profoundly crucial step to follow the wisdom of his own passion, empowering him to create one of America's great entrepreneurial success stories: a two billion dollar business called Starbucks.

Again, when it comes to following your passion and living your dream:

All degrees are absolutely essential, but essentially worthless.

Remember, Bill Gates had no sacred sheepskin. In all probability the lack of a college diploma would have disqualified him from working at most major American companies. Fact of the matter is, it probably would have made getting through any corporate door tough when he could not rely on the possession of a college diploma as the basic proof that he possessed a talent and intelligence. Which you can bet had a lot to do with the way Bill was treated when he tried to make his presentation to those wise gray heads at IBM.

Legend has it that like a baby born with a tail, Bill Gates was someone they couldn't get rid of fast enough. Probably watched with joy as they shoo-flyed him away. The point is, and again, I want to separate it here: There is nothing you can do or show new under their sun until you prove otherwise. Bill Gates learned this early on. So totally and completely great was his belief in his passion, that nothing, not anyone, could deter him from the grand wonders he wanted to create. Standing ovation for Billy boy. And as for IBM?

Shoulda, woulda, coulda . . .

Okay back to Ron and that first spring day of work, that he remembers clearly, as clearly today as then—that emotional beginning of being daisy-fresh with the preparation and background that would allow a career in the wine and spirits business to become a reality.

Ron had the schooling behind him, but better than that, he grew up around the business, and even much better than that, he knew a good deal of how to present the company's portfolio of offerings. His expectations were way high about the living he would make. This was no slim-shady Ponzi scheme. There was plenty of jack to be made, the dollars real and potentially many when he would begin calling on an account and pitch the industry's class of the field A+ brands. Ready to go like hell, Ron knew that there was nothing that could take him away from hitting the streets and triumphantly making his mark . . .

Unless, of course, Ron was taken to the Dead Room.

Now the Dead Room was a room that few had ever ventured to and even fewer ever dared volunteer to go. No way as cavernous as the warehouse space that stored the Canadian Club, Cutty, Jack Daniel's and the rest, the Dead Room, nevertheless, was in its own foreboding way, vast. It was here in exile, at the very back, behind a heavy paint-peeling steel door, that dead inventory was finally, unceremoniously, laid to rest. And who can tell what makes perfectly good inventory become a scourge? Ultimately, it's a combination of many unfortunate factors. But mostly, there's one fact that stands out from all the rest.

It doesn't sell.

Surely somewhere there must exist a Dead Room museum. A shrine dedicated to corporate America's consumer can't-misses. Over here, ladies and gentlemen, is the famous Edsel and on your right for your chuckling pleasure, who can of course forget: New Coke. And up ahead, a wonderful photo opportunity, the Sony Betamax. The Dead Room here, and for many

long months, was a temple honoring a stacked-up trib-
ute to someone's not so bright idea at Seagrams.

Banished.

Ron would have been crazy to think otherwise.
What else would you call it when your whole life, every
prior experience, all the years of preparation was for,
well, nothing? Born and bred to mine diamonds, Ron
was given a shovel and pointed at a pile of coal. And
while most would sag and drop into despair, all enthusiasm and energy seeping fast, the paranoia of youth ral-
lies against a world bent on tearing you down. Still,
rocked, still staring and still, well, somewhat stunned,
Ron confidently accepted the goddamn challenge, wondering how in the hell in this or any other universe he
was ever going to sell this shit. That was the thought
that kept him company.

That and the specter of failure.

But being a child of the Pepsi generation, there were
a lot worse things than this, and that's the kind of lie
Ron told himself: I'll show them, now and forever show
them all, if they give me one half a chance. Which, in
point of fact, is what they *did* give. That and oh, just one
more thing . . .

A spanking brand new salesman's sample case. An
undodgeable truth, filled with bottles of hopeless dead
stock from the even more hopeless Dead Room, a case
weighted with the impossibility of any success.

Jaded, full of scars from the marketplace, the tired
ancients watched, all seven of them, and generously im-

parted the Solomon wisdom of their many years. . . . *Hey kid, don't lug that thing around, you'll grow a hump.* . . . was the first nugget from the woolly mammoths, followed closely by . . . *Your hand will turn into a claw.* . . . *Take a brochure, show 'em a picture.* . . .*Why go kill yourself?* . . . *No one can sell that shit anyway.* And now, looking back on it, do you want to know what the strongest memory of that day was?

They were right. But they were wrong.

Wrong by cases and cases of the dead inventory, which is what Ron sold that very first day out. And after all these many years who can remember what the case count was the next day or the next day after that, or in all the quick days that followed, as he went about nailing down sale after sale, but by the second week's end you could happily go make plans to turn the Dead Room into a bowling alley, if you wanted to, that's how out from under all that inventory empty the Dead Room had become.

Amazing?

To the ancients anyway. But only to them. They were a wise and experienced bunch, still they could not believe that the debris carted in the heavy-as-stone salesman's sample case had—miraculously out of some bizarre blue—sold. That said, would they believe that what was *really* being carried in the salesman's sample case was the same substance that was carried in Ron's head, heart and soul?

Unlikely.

Would they believe that even if the case was laden with bricks it would still feel light as a feather, because—and here more important than anything, is the very real secret about the case and why it was always carried close without the slightest hint of any effort—inside, alongside whatever its contents were…shhhh.

A like-what-you-do-life loaded with passion and burning desire.

Freely put, Ron loved being in sales.

And would the ancients be able to appreciate and understand that?

Doubtful.

Because truth being the truth, life had for so long now held them sour and captive, with no sense of contentment in their air. Years wrinkle the skin, but to live without a passion, well, that wrinkles the soul. Tired and exhausted, the grizzled warriors viewed the days hunkered in their foxholes, disgusted with their circumstances, bitter about the path not taken, their true gifts and talents squandered. Worse. Their regrets had taken the place of their dreams. Worse yet. Their desires had forever been set aside, and perhaps even more tragic, all but forgotten. Trapped. Totally. The ancients watched the years, wondering what it must be like to do what you like and to like what you do, and why would someone young—*anyone*—want to share their chains?

Pretty withering.

And pretty thought-provoking too, when filed away as a lesson. And do please file it. Tattoo it in back of your eyelids. Sneak a reassuring peek whenever. It can save your ass many times over when the echo of doubt comes ringing. Make it part of your mantra: real happiness in life depends on how you embrace what you are passionate about. Only by embracing your passions can you achieve the satisfaction and joy in life you are destined for.

Now, a word here should probably be added about how hard it is to make what is known in the great game of business as The Cold Call. Actually two words.

Very hard.

Not hard like climbing Everest or swimming the Atlantic. We're talking hard like roof tarring or asphalt slinging on a steamy August afternoon. It is agonizing, miserable work with the cloud of rejection over you every time you set out. And it never goes away, no clearing skies. And if that were not enough, throw in the additional always present pressure of failure and some, many, most, all, have a hard time dealing with it. A fair number can't deal with it at all. Ahhhhh, but for the ones who do hang in and hang on, for the ones who believe in themselves and believe and find joy in what they are doing, the ones that pursue their passion, you will need a calculator to add up the rewards of their perseverance.

Remember, no successful person ever made it without facing the risk of rejection and failure. More importantly, remember that the word *risk* often is accompanied by the word *no* as its constant companion. But without ever risking rejection and failure, you will never hear the word *yes*. By having the courage to risk rejection and failure, you provide yourself with the wondrous opportunity to succeed. More about this later.

But for now, another important aside. A short one, promise.

Business people are constantly getting pummeled from every direction. They take an incredible amount of shit compared to regular human beings. No matter how much you've read, heard or imagined, a career in business, *any* business, is really, primarily, finally, about one thing.

The next sale.

Doesn't matter who you are selling, or if what you are selling has the potential to change lives. The simple and plain truth of the matter is this: nobody wants to take the time from their busy day to see or hear what they regard as another pestering pitch. Nothing personal, it goes with the territory, but remember again: with increasing import, there is nothing you can do or show new under their sun until you prove otherwise.

And if you're lucky, skilled and shrewd enough to open a few doors, then you better be prepared to seize the opportunity and dazzle. Dazzle brilliantly. Create an excitement, dispense enthusiasm about whatever it is you bring—an idea, a plan, a product, a service—it doesn't matter. Trumpet it assiduously with passion and propensity; let the light into their world, the point being:

You are not Columbus setting sail on uncharted waters; you are Captain Average navigating through a sea of sameness, unless you show them that you are different.

Keyword: Show.

Something. Everything.

When you go out there, and forever after, show them your best. Show vitality, a fervor, an exuberance, an energy, a galvanizing passion and power that can carry the day. Most importantly, show them the illumination of a person who is d-i-f-f-e-r-e-n-t—different because he/she has the mettle to recognize their own true talents and believes in, no, strike that, not believes, *lives* their passions! A Zen proverb illustrates this point: *Within the sacred space of your being, clarity and radiance will shine, and as you allow yourself to shine, your world becomes a more glorious place.*

Enter: you.

Now there is a tendency in books of this kind to page out some standard how-to bullshit stuff about survival strategies for the businessman/businesswoman—pep-rally linear-minded manage-yourself guides to build a successful resume to help you land a better job, how-to-triumph advice for dot com babies and wannabe deal achievers. Much to-do babble about "skilling" your way outside the box, dressing for success, thinking strategically, growing professionally and inspiring shared vision . . . blah blah blah. That's all round-mouth, square-deal tossed salad, and we're not going to fiddle with the reality of that world.

Forget it.

Forget the pop and fizz of those quick fix, how-to guru manuals on the business and self-help bookshelves that tell you how to develop a full-court press to climb the ladder.

Hey, we're sounding reveille here; you've already got the job. Believe it! You are CEO of the most important company on earth. Let's call it, YOU Inc. A one-person venture that specializes in self-optimization, with the explicit objective of succeeding in bringing to the world, through your passion, the special talents and gifts that are uniquely *you*. And make no mistake, it's a full-time, twenty-four-seven, fifty-two weeks, a lifetime position. It doesn't matter if you're twenty-three years old, or forty-three years old, if you work for someone else or own your business, even if you don't work at all. Again, doesn't matter. What *does* matter is that you have plunked down dollars on this book, hoping to gain a little help obtaining a more empowering, productive, joyous and successful life. The kind of life that you, we, all, truly long for.

And do you know how hard that is?

Well it is. Goddamn hard. And forget those happily-ever-after Hollywood horseshit endings like Jimmy Stewart and *It's A Wonderful Life*. It's not a wonderful life; it's just life, unless you make it wonderful by tapping and rediscovering the incredible source of intuitive wisdom, creativity and talent deep within you.

And that's what this book is about, really, the power and the empowerment of you.

Pssst. Listen.

Bring the book up. Get close to the page.

Closer.

This is important.

Ready?

YOU ARE SPECIAL!

You are the product of millions of years of evolution, making you a unique combination of gifts and talents. There has never been anyone like you before and there will never be anyone like you again. What you feel, what you dream, is sooo different from what anyone else feels and dreams.

You are here for a reason.

You were born with an innate capability to do, be and have all that your heart yearns for. There is something you are supposed to be doing and you mustn't waste another day ignoring it. And that's what we want you to get out of the many pages yet to come: a realization that in order to be truly happy, to be completely fulfilled, you need to live a life designed around your own special talents and gifts. No dream is impossible if you just dare to live it. You must, underline *must*, live your life and not someone else's. And so comes the question.

Are you?

If not, then get moving.

Success at life comes when you achieve a more fulfilling and gracious existence, by catching and living the dream that you absolutely deserve to live. Only then will you triumph and walk the days with the kind of real happiness and satisfaction that come as a result of embracing what you are passionate about.

How long have you been ignoring your desires or living with the pressure to be someone else? Now is the time to tend to *you*, allowing yourself to believe in the dream and in you, the dreamer. By attaining clarity on what really matters most to you in your life, you will possess the quintessential power to turn your dream into a reality and achieve the happiness you are truly destined for. Whatever Dead Room you find yourself in, remember that it is you who has the key that can open the door to your greatest good.

Flashback. (Your turn to summon up the years.)

Okay, class. You're young. Very. The song was easy and fun to sing and the message carried, the single best thing. Remember?

Row, row, row your boat, gently down the stream. Merrily, merrily, merrily, merrily—

Did you fill in the blank?

Good.

Turn the page.

Let's get started . . .

JI ZHONG

Chapter Two
STAY FOCUSED

SCREECHIE, SCHWARZENEGGER AND STALLONE

The snow goose need not bathe

to make itself white.

—Lao-Tzu

Ask any of the Hollywood powers that be to provide a list of the most popular bankable box-office draws, not only in America, but in the world, and at the very top of their pick, year after year, will be Arnold Schwarzenegger and Sylvester Stallone.

Theirs have been and are now, without argument, genuinely remarkable careers that have had a consistent hold on the public's fancy, made their studios many hundreds of millions of dollars, and provided each of them with phenomenal fame and fortune—all this despite one very obvious and simple truth:

They can't act.

Now, that's not to imply that they don't have the talent or the intelligence or the ability. Clearly, they are wonders, great stars. Let us not forget that Stallone lifted himself from far-fetched obscurity to amazing Academy Award®–winning success by writing and starring in *Rocky*. Still, he would be the first to proclaim he hasn't the genius of an Olivier. And if you think for one second that Schwarzenegger believes he can compete with Anthony Hopkins for parts, or that Adam Sandler is pleading with his agent to arrange an audition for Othello, or that Madonna is certain she can out-warble Whitney or Striesand, forget it. In their dark nights, away from the adulation and the entourage, when their heads hit the pillow, in their heart of hearts they know the true unvarnished breadth of their gifts and what it took to get them to where they are.

They know.

They lived it in the beginning, and to some extent they live it still. And can you imagine how the conversations went with family and friends whenever the crossroads question came . . .

So Sylvester/Arnold what are you going to do with yourself?

Silence. Finally the illuminating linguistics would come: "*I wanna be an actah,*" from Sly. And from Arnold, same thing, only his was, "*I want to be an acht-or.*"

And, of course, my guess here is that the inevitable response to the madness of their answer wasn't, "*Great! Fabulous! You'll show that Paul Newman!*" It was no doubt more likely a look of "*what are you nuts?*" disbelief. Because before Sly transformed his physique into a beautiful chiseled work of art and the doctors did the same for the features of his face, he was just another no-way New York street kid that you had to strain an ear to understand. And in case anyone is interested, Arnold's looks are a whole lot easier on the eyes now too; just check out his earlier work. But still, before he summoned all the talent he possessed to tell the world "*I'll be back*" he had to *get* there first, which was such an unbelievable no-chance long shot that the Hollywood high strata still shake their heads in befuddled amazement.

Point?

An important one, and it is this:

Superstardom has made Schwarzenegger and Stallone the emperors of glory you see up on the screen today. But it was always more than anything else the power of their passion, the unquestionable hard driven desire, commitment, stamina and steadfast focus to live their dream that *got them there.*

Same with Screechie.

Like Schwarzenegger and Stallone, Screechie too is one of life's shining superstars. Not that hysterical fans and paparazzi happily line up for hours to catch a glimpse. But truth to tell, a picture of Screechie is worth a thousand words, and I know this because Screechie brought a few of his wonderful Polaroids to our twenty-year high-school reunion. And there was a considerable scramble to peek at these pictures from those of us who grew up hanging with Screechie.

Why?

In the early years, Screechie was considered a handful.

Which was cause for more than many a concerned headshake from the adults, because Screechie came from a highly respected well-to-do family. His father was a very successful doctor with a specialty in pulmonology, his mother—no Brady Bunch mom—had a degree in tax law, and when you were an only child coming from an environment like that, at the very least, tremendous expectations framed you.

In their eyes, Screechie was, of course, a vein of gold.

His future greatness a certainty, his parents went to grand lengths to insure him more than a solid chance of endless opportunities. From the very beginning, then through grammar, middle and on into high school, so lofty were their hopes, so solid their rock of belief that nothing could—should—ever slow Screechie down, that they happily handed him keys to a beautiful black shiny showroom new Camaro Z.

And okay, while many would question the soundness of such a gift for a sixteenth birthday, those of us who were barely shaving didn't question it at all. We were all crazy with the way coolness of it, as we piled into it that very first day, rocking a cassette into the tape player, howling with glee as Screechie would grip the wheel, wait for the traffic light to turn green, then pop the clutch, *screeeech* the Goodyears, flashshift the thing quick into second, screech them again and when third gear came, causing the tires to magically smoke and screech the pavement unbelievably again, *bingo*—the legend of Screechie was then and forever delivered to our tiny world.

Sweet memories, those days.

Anyway, the seasons changed and, alas, so did we. And as the many months brought us closer to graduation and the gearing up for college, the once pristine, now road-beat Cammy drove Screechie further away. He had no use for school, said it many times. Meant it.

Screechie's parents, to put it mildly, fell into despair.

We all heard bits and pieces of the pitched battle, Screechie telling us about the war that was raging between him and his parents, the arguments blasting away. Because for good or ill, Screechie let fly that he had different feelings and interests concerning his life. And when they said *this* and he said *that* and they said they didn't want to hear not a bit of it, that was fine with him, he didn't care, he just didn't care, because his mind was definitely without any question made up.

Which clearly set Screechie's parents off.

Big time.

Because they had their dreams wrapped up in Screechie. They made a pact from before the day of his birth that he would want for nothing. And as he grew they gave as much of their time as their time would allow, doing all they could, always going the extra mile to offer him not only the material things but the never-ending emotional support to go along with them. So, when Screechie was seven and he came in from the playground to tell them he wanted to be an army man, his parents smiled and pat him on the head. And when he was nine and told them he was going to be a rootin-tootin cowboy, his parents beamed and told him that he would make the best cowboy. But when Screechie was pushing seventeen and announced first chance he got that he was going to bust a move to someplace tropical and live a life enjoying the surf and sky, well it was hard for them to continue to extol his brilliance. Because if Screechie didn't understand by this time that medicine was his future, obviously they were doing something wrong.

Screechie didn't understand.

And they were doing something wrong.

Now, gang, the object here is not to go point a finger. There is no right side.

Screechie was clearly pent up and rebellious, questioning authority, struggling for satisfactory answers, and when you're a young man of seventeen on the brink of manhood that's your job. And who can brand blame on parents who wanted more for their child than a life of work showing up at the brick factory?

Still, as I said, and I am serious, Screechie's parents were doing something wrong. Not that they were alone in this practice, which by the way, there is a term for.

Care to take a guess what it is?

Wait. I'll give you a hint.

It probably has changed the life of a friend; maybe it has changed your life.

Got it?

Take it from me, you don't know. Not your fault. Because it happens so goddamn often that it goes unnoticed until it's too late. In a blink, you're the next casualty. Anyway, it's responsible for a lot of unhappiness, and believe me, it would take a computer a while to number how many people who have been affected.

Another hint. It's two words. The initials of the two words are D and K. Anybody got a clue yet? My bet is still no. Enough with the hints, let me help you along. Because to be fair and honest the term isn't even in the dictionary.

Ready?

The term is Dream Killing. There. That's it. Were any of you close? Probably not. Now let me tell you precisely what it means.

Except I can't.

Like I said, it's not in any dictionary. But if it was, and I think it should be, this is how I think it should be defined:

Dream Killing; to put an end to, or to destroy, a fond hope, idea or desire.

And that's what a parent does to a child. Under the well-meaning, good-intentioned guise of dutiful parenting, they become guilty of dream killing.

How, though?

Good question.

Why?

Ditto.

But to eyeball in on the answers we would have to devote many pages here to a shrink circle, letting the psychologists and psychiatrists spiel on and on all they want.

Yikes. Collective cringe all around, right?

Instead, let me offer a positional concept of Freud's, one that all these educated mavens now agree on at least in theory, and it is this: All healthy children seem to display inbred qualities of certain desires and talents beyond their comprehension. Recognizing these capacities and knowing how to cultivate their full potential can be the difference between those of us who are successful and happy, and those of us who are not.

It is this beginning emotional focus that is chipped away from children at an early age by parents and teachers, continually fractured out of them through adolescence, so that by the time they are adults, they are as unfulfilled and as prosaic as their elders.

Studies show remarkably, even shockingly, that in the first five years of life we as children are told *no* over fifty thousand times and *yes* only five thousand times. This foundation of conditioning is how children are trained to conform and succeed. The minute percentage of the victims who escape this fate become the rare minority that go on and change the world.

So, if somewhere there is a Gina who displays a genuine talent for drawing or design, well, that may make the little darling a source of family pride; but what's that got to do with the reality of her making a living in today's modern world? And if John begins his senior high-school year with a clear ambition to become a fireman, nothing wrong with that; but if it's lives you want to go about saving, then study hard and be a doctor.

The fact is, college is not for everyone.

The drag is, a formidable paternal presence pushes the SATs.

And so it goes.

And I don't think that this can be pointed out too often, which is why I want to point it out again. There are no villains, no spilled blood in all of this—just pressure placed upon us by others that keeps our dreams from being discovered, our passions from being pursued.

But you have to add this: we let it happen.

How many of you know of or have friends who have gone through or are gamely going through the motions, forsaking their true gifts and dreams because of outside circumstances and forces? If you do, ask them about the road not taken.

But for now please listen. The truth is simply this:

It's your life. You are in charge!

If there is one thing more important than any other one thing in this book, that is it.

Again, for emphasis—

YOU ARE IN CHARGE!

You are the only one who can change your life! In order to achieve and succeed you must recognize that your only true commitment is being true to yourself. You must be the relentless architect of your own unique possibilities. You must have the guts, the persistence and (remember?) the passion, to do everything you can to fight like hell to stay focused. Make it your war cry to stay focused, avoiding the often subtle and not so subtle powers and forces which will pull you off your true path and away from your deserved hopes and ambitions.

Practice the ancient all-important art of *wishcraft*. What I mean by this is keep your focus on the goals and dreams that the real you *wishes* to achieve. Shun the traps and trips that others would lay on you. Listen to your heart and believe in your ability to create a happy, meaningful life regardless of outside factors or pressures imposed upon you by the needs and wishes of others.

In plain English, quit bitching about your life and do something about it! You have the power within you to make your dreams come true, but unless you take action, unless you commit to *focus on what truly matters to you*, nothing will change. As long as you are alive on this planet, whatever you can do or dream you can begin it. You can make it happen! Puh-leese, make it happen. Because, in this world you only get an allotted span, and you're the one who has to look in the mirror at age sixty!

So if there's an artist, a dancer, an actor, a musician, a person who loves to sell, a business owner or an entrepreneur inside you longing to come out, do yourself a solid—free your gifts and create a life you will love. When you do what you are, you will love what you do. Stay focused on your dream, moving forward and ahead with undiminished optimism. To be truly happy, to be completely fulfilled you must stay focused on what you want for you. So take a moment right now, and ask yourself in total honesty, *Are you living your life or are you living someone else's?*

Think about it.

I'll give you a half a minute or so, during which time

I'll tell you briefly about how time "buried" our good friend Screechie.

To all of us, anyway.

We lost every trace of Screechie after he finally relented, agreeing to give college a try and put off Armageddon with his parents for a few months. The time spent on campus was a miserable quagmire for Screechie, so when he traded the Camaro Z for a fly Harley and headed off for some faraway hell-and-gone place, it had finally become immediately clear—even to his parents—that there was little anyone could do at all.

So we left the legend there.

Done.

At any rate, not much thought was given to Screechie during those next passing months. Truth to tell, the most fortunate of us were busy with our own ecology shifting, dealing with the experiences of dorm life and campus life and the mindless freedoms that life in general offered us at that age. It wasn't until many, many months later that we heard with genuine horror that time had taken Screechie to the nightmare of Vietnam. The news jarred me out of orbit and my thoughts went immediately to that colorful kid who wanted to be an army man and then a cowboy; and with fingers very much crossed, I feared for his safety, cursing him with real sadness for not ending up enjoying the surf and sky as he had vowed.

Madness.

But now with my mind moving forward a bit, and

back to my high-school reunion, I can report the real joy I had when I saw the legend standing there.

I won't bore you with the unimportant grace notes about all who were in attendance, the jabber about who looked good, who didn't, who put the poundage on, which men blew their feathers and got bald, which women were time warps, desperately hanging on to youth that was mostly gone. If you were interested in that sort of dish, there was plenty enough juicy gossip to keep you going. But the real talk was about Screechie, overwhelmingly.

About how healthy and fit and genuinely contented he appeared. And I don't know of any other way that better illustrates what they were all babbling so happily about than to describe the half dozen or so pictures that Screechie had brought:

There was Screechie, standing tall, the army chopper pilot with many years spent serving our country and wearing a uniform full of heroic medals to prove it. The next series of photos were a real hoot, capturing Screechie the cowboy, living a Levi-clad life with his wife and children in Bozeman, Montana. And I'll always remember where my mind went as I stood sharing Screechie's wondrous Polaroids with those crowding around me.

The thing of it was, what we all were realizing then and there was, that unlike most in attendance, with Screechie there was no phoniness. Not a phony bone in his body. He was, truly, what he always wanted to be.

Himself.

Now it's been, amazingly, another ton of years since that reunion and when we got to writing this particular part of the book, we were obviously curious about how Screechie was making out. So before we began to fill the pages, we set about looking up the legend, made a few calls and guess what? Remarkably, we found him without much difficulty at all. And if you would like to know what he is up to now, you can find him just as easily too.

Enjoying the surf and sky.

In Kahului, Maui, Hawaii.

What he is doing, well, I almost came out of my chair I was so excited—he's the principal owner of one of Hawaii's premier helicopter tours. Each and every day his state-of-the-art helicopters provide spectacular views of one of the earth's most breathtaking paradises. And after contacting him I don't know whether I was more pleased than surprised or more surprised than pleased.

Unimportant.

What was important for me, then and now, is that the legend of Screechie continues to remain magical. More important, still, is the marvelous gift his life provides—that to live your dream, you don't need to change yourself, you need only to change your life. Finally, and by far the most important lesson of all is that life is an adventure. Your adventure.

And it's up to you to play the starring role.

It's up to you to make your life story into what you want it to be. Your dream can and will come true if you focus on your desire to go from where you are to where you want to be.

Look, get yourself geeked. Don't just make up your mind to push yourself to be a success at life; you have to make up your mind to pull yourself too. Lao-Tzu said, *"The snow goose need not bathe to make itself white."* Neither need you do anything but be yourself. Focus on who you are and what you are capable of, resisting the strong pressure from family and friends and the self-imposed limits that may prevent you from opportunities for personal fulfillment and achievement. Eliminate the things you are tolerating and that are draining your energy. Stop putting up with what's dragging you down. Command an unending supply of perseverance that will allow you to break through barriers and achieve top billing in the story of your life. Please remember, your success and happiness are literally just an act away. Focus with ferocity on being what you want to be, doing what you want to do and having what you want to have . . .

And value who you are and what you want . . .

And act as if there are no limits to what you can achieve . . .

And maintain an attitude of gratitude for who you truly are . . .

And take responsibility for yourself to accomplish your dreams . . .

And stay focused on your goals in order to attain them . . .

And remember that other people's expectations for you do not have to become your reality . . .

And play the role you were destined to play . . .

And make it a performance of a lifetime . . .

And . . . and . . . and enough with the ands. Just one last thing.

Serious stuff.

Never, never *ever* no matter what, give up on mining the gift and talent you've been given. These are qualities that will open the doors to the infinite possibilities of your life. Stay focused on who you are and what you want to be, and in the end you too will become a shinning superstar in the theater of life . . .

Like Screechie, Schwarzenegger and Stallone.

LAO SHI

Chapter Three
FIND A MENTOR

IT TAKES ONE
TO KNOW ONE

From the pine tree learn of the pine tree.

And from the bamboo of the bamboo.

—Zen Proverb

Here is how you live your dream (tidied up a tad for print):

You break your ass.

You don't buy a lottery ticket. You don't rub a magic lamp. And most of all, you don't wait for the Publisher's Clearing House prize patrol or anybody else to come knocking at your door with a silver platter. For the umpteenth time, the whole mother number one thing is—please believe it—it is crucially and primarily up to each and every one of us to make our lives into what we want. In other words:

Git jiggy wit it and rock the house.

Get cranking on a course that will move you toward your goals by practicing your ABC's.

No, not those ABC's.

These ABC's: Action, Belief and Clarity. Let's call them the ABC's of Personal Responsibility.

All right class, some advice.

A small piece.

It be a good idea to take a little time to skull pack this stuff.

Ready?

A is for Action. Create a sense of urgency so your mind will organize a plan of action to move you toward your goals and dreams. Many/most have the burning desire to make something happen in their lives. They are filled with ambition but don't know what to do with their energy. They don't know how to act upon it. You must take responsibility to empower yourself to accomplish your own desires. This can only be achieved through actions based on a strong sense of your own self-worth, a willingness to take risks, and the emotional courage to journey outside your comfort zone. By mobilizing your mind, you activate powerful and purposeful motivation that can overcome and lift you up, up and away from living in what Ron and I call the polluted doubt and uncertainty of *Atmosfear*—the fear of failure; the fear of rejection; the fear of what family, friends and colleagues might think; the fear of being different and, paradoxically, the fear of success. You must not allow your fears to keep you from living your dream. You must take control of your life and what you want for yourself once and for all. You must look, talk, think and act like the person you want to become. Your future is not determined by luck, it's determined by the actions you take each and every day. Successful people do the things that unsuccessful people are not willing to do. You must take action. You can and you *will* catch and live your dream, but you have to act! Remember, A is for Action. It's also for energy, intensity, inner strength, responsibility, change, initiative, courage, daring and persistence.

B is for Belief. Believe in who you are and what you are capable of. Build a solid personal foundation and demonstrate a strong confidence in your strengths, skills and talents. Unless you believe you are one hundred percent deserving of your dreams coming true, self-doubt and self-sabotage will get in your way. It's absolutely paramount for you to believe that today's dream is tomorrow's reality. Consciously know that you can overcome the fears that hold you back from going for the dream that you long for. Believe in your ability to create a happy, meaningful life, regardless of any outside circumstances. Believe that your hard work will make it happen. You can't be a wimpy, whining squid mope out there on the dream-seeking trail and overcome the obstacles that block your path. Know that the surest way not to fail is to believe that you will succeed! By believing in yourself you will endure the challenges. Believe you can and you will live your dream! Believe it! B is for belief. It's also for determination, endurance, commitment, resoluteness, direction, vision, inspiration and undiminished optimism.

C is for Clarity. Know your goals and dreams clearly, and focus on what needs to be done. Gain clarity on what is truly important to you, so you can create a clear and compelling vision of what you want most from life and how best to achieve it. Have the vision to recognize opportunities or to make your own. Be aware of what you need to do. Stay focused on what you want and remove yourself from people, things or situations that confine or drain you. See past the clutter and confusion that may limit your success. Seek more than others think is wise. Risk more than others think is safe. Know that the only limitations in life are the ones you place on yourself. Maintain a clear vision of what you want to do and be, so that you can live a future based on your goals, desires and aspirations and not those of others. Make it perfectly clear; you can and you will catch and live your dream! C is for Clarity. It's also for attention, focus, balance, concentration, sense of self, perception, intuition, awareness and consciousness.

Know this—your gifts and talents are only part of the equation. Putting into practice the ABC's of Personal Responsibility coupled with the act of choice will create and develop the catalyst for change.

In summation: Enthusiastically act on what you believe and ardently desire, and it will come true.

If you just groaned, thinking that taking that first step is a bitch, fair enough. This is why in life, we need all the help we can get, and we need it every step of the way.

So, here is another piece of advice.

Big piece.

Find a mentor.

A role model. No, wait. Hold up a sec.

Make that a *goal* model.

Find someone who is doing what you want to be doing. A been-there, done-that person whose experience, career and wisdom can help you learn to succeed.

Mentors demonstrate how much is possible. Whatever it is you want to be or do, there is already somebody who is being it or doing it. Think about those high performance people whose careers and lives you admire, in whose footsteps you would like to follow. Think about what they can add to your reality by telling you how to get started and what to expect along the way. Then think about this: If you are willing to be an appreciative student, know that you'll be pleasantly surprised to find that most successful individuals wouldn't mind being a Yoda.

It's true. Most people who have achieved a certain degree of success also have a wonderful sense of career guidance. They are willing to share the kind of advice that may contribute to the growth, development and wish fulfillment of an aspiring Jedi. The act of mentoring—to be elevated to the position of a Solomon—allows the mentor to repay in some way the intrinsic benefits he/she has derived from their success. These successful people have often been helped by mentors of their own, and are desirous to return the favor to the world. They want to offer help.

And if you're going "Mentor-shmentor, what goddamn good is a mentor when I don't even know how to get started on what I'm trying to do?" Well, the answer lies in the question. As Yoda, the mighty Jedi Master once said, "Try not. *Do*. Or *do not*. There is no try." That being said, how about we drag your butt back from the Dark Side.

Okay, let's start by flipping back a couple of pages and going over the ABC's of Personal Responsibility again. And then again. And don't hesitate to refer back to them again once more whenever you find yourself starting to drift from your goals and dreams. Make them your mantra. Especially A. And for good reason. To make a difference you must commit yourself to act, to *do*. In the words of Nike: *Just do it!* The simple fact that you must never forget is that only you can know what your dream means to you, so only you are able to make yourself do what it takes to achieve it. In order for things to happen, you have to be somebody who *makes* things happen. And at the top of your list, the very first action you need to do as soon as it is humanly possible is to hitch your wagon to a mentor, a like-minded individual who can nurture your dream and your well-being by pointing the way to a smooth path or by helping you find the path, simply by offering himself as tangible evidence of what one can become. An ancient Zen proverb states: *If a poet, show them your poem. If a warrior, show them your sword.*

The experience and intellectual engagement of mentors can guide you to new ideas and perspectives. Their life lessons can challenge you to move beyond your perceived limits, suggesting more effective and focused actions. Through a mentor you will immediately begin to value more who you are and what you want.

So let's set to work trying to find a mentor.

Once again, a mentor is someone who is simply

willing to offer the kind of support and guidance that can help you develop the necessary skills and knowledge that will allow you to become your best self. A mentor is someone who can offer you wisdom without prejudice, someone who inspires you to greater achievement, by providing you with ideas and concepts that go beyond your experience. A mentor can be a teacher, a coach, a counselor, a role-type model, a neighbor, a friend or even a relative.

Briefly now, an example:

There once was a small nine year old who was driven by an almost impossible dream: to one day shoot hoops in the NBA. He spent hours, weeks, months and years growing up talking, practicing and playing basketball in backyards, at the Y, in city parks, in pick-up games, one on one, that sort of thing. When his waking hours were given to sleep there were always the dreams where he would, to the screams and cheers of the crowd, make the last winning spectacular shot of the game. And when he wasn't all the time staying glued to polishing his skills, he could still be seen dribbling or holding a ball in his hands, sometimes gripping the roundness with his fingers, getting the feel, always remembering the advice that in basketball you weren't going anywhere if you didn't have the feel. All the years made him good but not, no one needed to tell him, great; still when the moment came for the final player selection of his high-school team, he was devastated to be quickly and without thought cut by the coach and told that he didn't make the team because the talent wasn't there. And as tragic as that seemed, it would have been *more* tragic still had his father not been there to mentor him—to offer the solid support, patience, motivation and enthusiasm and to provide the power behind the belief that his son could and *would* achieve his dream. Together, the father as mentor and the son as mentee, they continued their powerful relationship, believing, persevering and plugging away on having, being and doing what the son wanted in life. As a result the world was able to experience the given gifts and talents of—according only to everyone—the greatest roundballer ever to play the game: Michael Jordan.

Now, the purpose of this example as well as the ones to follow is to show that finding a mentor may be much easier than you think. The wisdom and encouragement of like-minded individuals is available to you, but in order to take advantage of this wealth of knowledge, you have to think, and act, and most of all, *do*. And just what does that mean, class?

Means you have to hustle.

So, take a few secs and ask yourself who are the people you sincerely admire? Then make a list. Take the time to research everything you can about them. What is it about their careers, lives and accomplishments that act as a beacon for your personal desires and being? Think about it over and over. Maybe you'll luck out and know somebody who knows somebody who knows somebody that knows these people. If you do, you can ask for an introduction. If you don't, and you probably don't, write one of these people whom you admire, tell them who you are, why you are contacting them, and what it is that you want. Take a moment to explain intelligently why their guidance would be so important to you, how their input will help you clarify your purpose, values and goals. This shows that you are respectful and worth taking the time to talk with. And if you truly and honestly do all you can to make the effort to reach out and write a thoughtful serious letter, guess what?

Nothing will come of it.

Except rejection. And frustration. And disappointment—

And so what!

Means nothing. We've already devoted a lot of ink on paper telling you that in pursuit of your dream, the unfortunate truth is that you had better expect rejection, frustration and disappointment as your constant companion.

But again, so what? Means nothing.

And when you were a kid, you knew this. You knew that when your parents finally took the training wheels off your bike and you went wobbly down the walk for the first time on two wheels, fell off, and scraped your knees, you knew that it meant nothing. You knew that the deal was that you got back up on the thing and tried again and again, and in no time you were out riding with your friends like the wind. And the same applies here. Failing to catch and live your dream doesn't result from falling down, but rather from staying down. So slip out of that comfy toasty sweater of life, put on a very tough hide and keep at it. Write another letter to the next person on your list, and when all you hear back is zip, write another and another. Continue on down the line and if you find this to be an increasingly hard to do and painful process, good. It means that you are entering uncharted ground, introducing change, breaking free from habitual patterns, kicking and clawing your way out of your comfort zone.

Perseverance is the keyword here. Make yourself like the Energizer Bunny and keep going and going and going. . . . Remember, finding a mentor, someone who is succeeding or has succeeded in his or her career is i-m-p-o-r-t-a-n-t, because they can understand your expectations and offer the guidance and direction that can help you make the right choices.

Which is why when Academy Award® winner, TV and pop icon Cher sent her 1999 CD *Believe* to market, she, despite any of her past successes, knew better than anyone that at age fifty-two she was a little long in the tooth to know how to promote herself to the MTV crowd. So after much thought and research she decided to seek out the advice of one of the most famous names of the '90s, the highly visible and market-savvy rock star Marilyn Manson. Never mind that Manson's album and concert ticket sales are fair at best—his knack for promotion and publicity are considered priceless. He understood Cher's needs and expectations, and his counsel and direction both marveled and helped her, and the wind up result was that *Believe* became the biggest ever hit of her career, earning her for the first time a highly coveted Grammy.

Now I know that you're probably thinking, "Oh yeah right, thanks—Cher. Great example. No *way* am I going to be able to contact a rock star, or a famous actor or a successful business person." If that is what you are thinking, then put both hands back on the wheel. Do not pass Go. Do not collect two hundred dollars and proceed directly back again to the ABC's of Personal Responsibility. . . .

B is for belief. Provide yourself with the rock of belief you need to travel down the dream-seeking trail. Then start researching. Doesn't matter what your dream is, read, read, then read some more, all you can, on what you are interested in. Hit the library. Hit the Web. With the advent of the internet, there's a shitload of information out there that's available to you. For instance, if your dream is to be an entrepreneur, professional or business owner, get yourself in front of a computer and check out **www.score.org**. This is the website of a volunteer organization called S.C.O.R.E., the Service Corps of Retired Executives, a group of retired successful business people who help with business plans or the marketing of ideas. And while you're at it, key up **www.hardatwork.com** and check out the Mentor section. These are just a couple of many sources that offer support, ideas, strategies and information that can provide you with the cape and boots you need to get off the ground and soar.

If your dream involves the arts, you get the idea. You're a creative person possessing the special combination of talent and mind. Do your research and get creative. For example, you want to be a filmmaker? Do you know about **www.projectgreenlight.com** or **www.ifilm.com**? Talk about good stuff. Or write to a filmmaker and tell them who you are and what you want. Who would you write to? Set to work making your list. But be realistic; construct a list that gives you the best possible odds for success. Is George Lucas on the list? Probably not a good choice, too busy right now with more *Star Wars*. What about James Cameron? What about him—nothing. Just ever since he decided he had to show the ship hit the iceberg, he has become the director of the most commercially successful, highest-grossing box office film of all time and wouldn't give a nod in your direction. Same with Spielberg. Same with Scorsese. Same with a lot of those who would be found on your list.

But if you methodically and thoughtfully did your research you would know about the brilliant moviemaking minds of the Coen Brothers or John Sayles, important giants in American independent film. What about Daniel Myrick and Eduardo Sanchez, the out of nowhere first time writers/directors of a little ditty called *The Blair Witch Project*? Their small, out-of-pocket and shaky film got them the covers of both *Time* and

Newsweek, not to mention $250 million at the box office. But if you more than anything would love to be mentored by a very successful and admired filmmaker, then through your research you would absolutely know that Spike Lee is respected and lauded for his career guidance and help to countless Hollywood wannabes. Take action. Write Spike. He's somebody who makes things happen . . . and so are you.

Which brings us to the fact that everybody who has attained any measure of success in business or the arts gets letters from people seeking direction and advice. Here, without any trouble, is an example of just such a letter:

> Dear Ms. Abrams,
>
> We would like to take the liberty of contacting you regarding our desire to publish a book that we have co-written. As successful entrepreneurs we receive numerous invitations to make guest-lecture appearances at college business classes around the country. It is through this experience that we have discovered and addressed the need for a book that fortifies the brain, the heart and the soul with practical myth-exploding homespun lessons about how to achieve one's goals and dreams and live the life one is ready to live. We hold your unique experience and acuity in high regard and would like the opportunity to contact you again in hopes that you would be willing to provide us with your advice on how to proceed. Thanking you in advance for any time and courtesies that you may be able to extend.

Now you would think that a letter such as this would do some good the very first time out.

Didn't.

Didn't get anywhere the second or third time it was sent either.

Fact is, dozens of such letters and e-mails were doggedly sent to a diligently researched list of publishers and editors.

Didn't change anything.

Filled with passion and exuberance and the focused belief to make things happen, the action step was to *keep sending out the letter on and on* and never give up. And if you are wondering if they met with success, we're happy to report . . .

You are holding the answer in your hands.

Live to dream.
Dream to live.
Let the sphere of yin and yang combine.
Polishing consciousness true destiny emerges.
Having refined the luminous spirit,
I discover the ancient secret of happiness.

MAO XIAN

Chapter Four
RISK

RUNNING
WITH SCISSORS

Know what you know

and know what you don't know.

—*Confucius*

Fact:

We all live on the same blue marble that circles the same orbit that subjects each and every one of us to the same gravitational pulls.

Question:

Why do most of us plod the earth with feet firmly planted on the ground, while others take a very crucial step that allows them to soar high with their dreams?

The answer, of course, is simply this:

Risk.

Plainly put, risk is essentially the glue that binds us to the possibility of success. No successful person ever made it without tempting risk or taking chances; it's a statistical reality. If you want to make wonders, you have to have a willingness to take risks. More specifically, you must give yourself the courage and the capacity to step beyond what is comfortable, predictable, familiar and sure. Risk is the challenge of the unknown. And it is this challenging of the unknown that allows for personal growth and development of personal power. It is part of life's adventure, so don't spend your life avoiding it. Avoiding risk, not risking, being too careful results in a reverse risk: the risking of the prospect of happiness and success.

In other words, if you want to make changes in your life, if you want to overcome procrastination, self-doubt and fear, if more than anything else you aspire to live a richer, more exciting, more satisfying life by realizing your dream, you have to take the risk of turning the potential of opportunity into reality. You must develop a risk consciousness; become your own power source, attain an unmoored positive mind and be a possibility thinker. Recognize that taking risks means not only the possibility of losing something, but also the possibility of gaining what you truly value, need and want in your life.

The importance of risk-taking is not what you may *get* from taking a risk, but rather what you *become* because of taking it. Realize that risk-taking is a positive and much needed experience in and of itself, because taking risks will build intellectual and emotional confidence in your ability to accept and confront challenges, expand your horizons and help you reach your dreams or goals. Risk can represent a meaningful commitment, a tool to create a detailed blueprint of a future possibility. Embrace risk-taking as an opportunity to see and appreciate possibilities.

And to succeed.

As has already been pointed out, it is up to you to take the responsibility for your success. Truly. In your always-decreasing days, you will be more disappointed by the things that you *didn't* do than by the things that you did. So make smart risk-taking a part of your life, because:

Generally speaking, only those who risk something achieve something.

Ask any seven-year-old ball-playing Little Leaguer and they will tell you: you can't steal second base and keep your foot on first base. If you want to move forward, then you will have to take a risk. You must take a risk.

Warning.

This doesn't mean if you feel something is worth a shot you go ahead and throw caution to the wind—take a risk in a loaded sense.

Absolutely not.

Careless risk, reckless risk, is nothing more than an all-out, odds-against-you-ever-succeeding long-shot gamble. You must not, you cannot gamble with your future.

Smart risk-taking is a thoughtful, careful, well-planned, calculated action with the strong possibility of success. Be responsible in your decision-making process. Before taking a jump, consider the old adage: look before you leap. Be sure you realize the consequences of the risks you decide to take. Because, yes, success is better than failure, but know that after you leap there can be elation or despair. Clearly visualize all the possible outcomes of your decision. What could go wrong? What are the chances of a worst-case scenario?

What is the worst case scenario? How can you lessen your risk? Ancient Samurai teaching: *When you want to test the depth of a stream, do not use both feet.*

Important consideration.

Reduce your chance of failure by researching all the pertinent facts, gain knowledge and get as much control as possible over any possible outcome.

Another important consideration.

If you don't take the risk, ask yourself: what will you lose? What is the consequence of doing nothing?

Most important consideration of all.

What is your goal or dream? Are you skilled enough to succeed? In other very important words, is what you want for yourself—are your goals and wishes—a dream or a fantasy?

The fact is, just because you want something badly simply isn't enough.

Be dead honest. Do you have the talents, the gifts, the personality and the drive to be what you want to be—to do what you want to do? Do you have what it takes—can you take what you have—and seize the opportunity of fulfillment when it eventually—inevitably—presents itself? Are you dedicating the hard work and time necessary to find out what knowledge and skills will be needed in order for your dream to become a reality?

Think about that.

The point to the above is this: the best way to be a success at life and catch and live your dreams is to wake up to who you *are*. Take a personality inventory. Understand that you are as you are because the universe is as it is. Discover the talents and gifts that uniquely define and direct you to your cosmic duty. Your choice to shape your destiny is the single most paramount decision you will make in your lifetime.

Forget the koochie-koochie-you're-so-good blind admiration that has been drummed into your head from the playpen on and understand that the key to your success is to *examine yourself critically*. Learn how to maximize your strengths and minimize your weaknesses and with that in mind, get as close as you can to this:

It is more important to know what you should *not* be doing in life than to know what you should be doing.

Learn all you can about the life purpose that lies inside you—your internal government. Find out if you have the DNA that will allow your heart to soar your dream.

APTITUDE + ATTITUDE = ALTITUDE

Huddle up, boys and girls. Every good-looking waiter fantasizes about being Tom Cruise or Brad Pitt, but fantasizing ain't gonna make it so. And some would-be musician has songs in her head—but what if they suck? We are all different with different gifts that the fates have given us, awesome gifts that, hidden or known, abound in our personality inventory. Gifts that will bring us great success *if we allow it*.

So how does one go about investigating and aligning one's own unique gifts, talents, abilities and offerings?

Nothing magical. There are many sources that can provide you with a clearer and more focused sense of what will unleash the giant within and lead you down the road of success, if you are ready to take a test drive.

Promise you, one of the best test-drive investments you can make in turning your dream into a reality is to set about trying to take a personality assessment test.

Now if your first reaction is to mumble and go all crimped-face at the idea, consider this:

For the same bucks as a couple of college textbooks you can sit in the comfort of your own home and take a quick, comprehensive test that can help you make important career decisions based on the special mosaic of your true gifts and talents. Ron and I are very familiar with these types of tests, and one of the best offered is by a company called Caliper. We have taken the test ourselves and, no kidding, it can assess an individual's potential for success for virtually every position there is—from baker to banker to entrepreneur to artist. You can be totally sure this is an investment well worth making in yourself. They send you the test, you take it, send it back, then they quick send you the results. This is an A+ action step, class. Please take the time to gather further information—check them out on the web at **www.caliperonline.com**. And while this path of self-discovery may not be everyone's salvation, it can very well make all the difference in your world.

Another wonderful source of information online that can be of absolutely tremendous benefit in helping you choose your life is at **www.jobprofiles.com**. Here, been-there already experienced workers in every field imaginable on our good earth kick it around, sharing the rewards, the demands, the skills, the challenges and most important the advice on entering their fields. With a full range of categories (agriculture and nature, arts and sports, business and communication, construction, manufacturing, education, science and government, health, social services, occupations in retail and whole-sale)—Wow-oh boy!—a kindred spirit and celebration of your ideal interests are what can be found within this realm.

So *prepare*, that's the password we're giving. Because failure to prepare is preparing to fail. Confucius said, *"Know what you know and know what you don't know."* Make sure you have all the tools you will need to take action to actualize and build your dream into a reality. Work ceaselessly to hone and sharpen your skills. Accu-mulate knowledge, support, assistance, and control and be ready to take your rightful destiny to choose, to change, to achieve, to take the risk of turning challenges into opportunities to succeed.

Rule number 1: Know that accepting challenges will move you closer to your dream.

Rule number 2: When you don't think you can ac-cept the challenges, refer to Rule number 1.

Build your risk-taking confidence. Approach risk-taking in small steps until you are comfortable with larger ones. Once you learn to minimize the fears and uncertainty of risks, subsequent and larger risks become easier to take. Start the process. Realize that the best angle from which to approach risk is the *try-angle*. When you can face the possibility of failure you take a tremendous step forward to making an unrelenting commitment to your dream.

What else? Just this: One way or another, do something. Anything to get your willingness-to-risk ball rolling. Cross a street against the red. Talk out of turn. Go full blast running with scissors. After all, in the final analysis, when all is said and done:

What have you got to lose. . . . but everything to gain.

Let the dream be present
and you will become genuine.
Let it guide you and you will flourish.
Let it become a reality and you will
become one with the Universe.

MU BIAO

Chapter Five
SET GOALS

WRITE

AWAY

One who moves mountains

begins by carrying away small stones.

—Zen Proverb

A brief refresher.

Because if you want to avoid banana peels along the dream-seeking trail, it's more than a good idea to go once more over what it takes to turn your dream into a reality. So, good people, take a moment to spark your memory. Freely summon up again and again what we've previously paged, and allow what has been presented to make a cameo appearance in your daily life. Dedicate yourself to: desiring what you deserve . . . doing what you want to do . . . being what you want to be . . . going where you want to go . . . living the life that is yours. And while you're at it: dream big dreams . . . polish the possibilities . . . believe, believe, believe! And to all of this you can add:

Pack a pencil.

Or a pen, or a beauty color Crayola, or whatever else you may want to use to write down your goals. But by all means, write them down! Because you can absolutely bank on the fact that this is the easiest and most powerful action step you can take toward achieving your dream.

Realize something: putting your goals in writing makes them real. By clearly identifying what you want, both your conscious and subconscious mind will adjust your thinking process, regarding the written message as a focus and not merely a daydream. Your thought processes will continuously be alert to situations and opportunities that can further your goal. There is a Buddhist saying: *We are what we think. With our thoughts we make the world.* It doesn't matter if you scribe using a stick in the dirt or a Palm Pilot. By writing down your goals you create a contract with yourself, documenting and increasing your personal commitment to shaping and defining them.

The reality is essentially this: when you write down your goals you are no longer thinking about your dream, you are *doing something about it*. You are taking a *positive action* by creating a graphic signpost that will act as a forceful, motivating visual to help you travel the path to success. Mainly, a written goal puts within your mind's eye a vision of a well-defined direct route to your specific destination. A map that will move you from your block of life and help take you where you want to go.

But you have to write it down. On a piece of paper. In one complete sentence. Precisely. Passionately. Powerfully. And most crucially:

Positively.

Every morning when you rise and every evening before you turn in, write down in a sharp, clearly defined, positive way, what it is that you want for yourself and write it down in the present tense.

If your goal is to run your own business, then believe the hell out of it and write it down: *I own my own business.*

If your goal is to be a computer game designer, same thing, write down *I am a computer game designer.* Notice that you do not see the words *I wish* or *I hope* or *I want to be*—rid these phrases from your lexicon. When you renovate your belief system by writing the goal as if it has already been attained, you will feel the emotions stir inside you, the passion and the zeal that come from the small simple action of pushing the pencil and writing your dream, visualizing your achievement, imagining your life.

There is a point to the paragraphs above and it is this: personal development experts will tell you that if you study successful people (and they do) you will find that since forever, they share a similar distinctive quality. This quality is their ability to create a vision, a template that shapes their lives, allowing them to determinedly no-stone-unturned stay focused on that vision, clinging to their truth until it becomes a reality.

The picture should be coming clear: written goals are the first step in developing a positive plan of action. Non-written goals are a jagged line that often result in little or no motivation; they are easy to put off, likely, in fact, to be tanked in the daily shuffle and unrealized.

One dull pencil is worth two sharp minds.

When you write down your goals, you can look at what you've written and ask yourself, *What will I do/*

what have I done today to get closer to my goals? By doing this, you are not allowing the career cripplers and dream killers to determine your life.

Another reminder. Because it can't be overemphasized enough, waaaaaay important. Remember always: *It's you who live above the store and have the power to create and control your own destiny.* Once you believe that, truly, the smell of success is very much in the air.

So, again for weight, hoping that we're preaching to the converted, write your goal down and then . . .

Break it down.

Into smaller and smaller sub goals or tasks, which when accomplished allow you to achieve your major goal or dream.

By breaking your overall goal down into these smaller parts, you greatly increase your ability to actualize the success you define. Focusing on these smaller goals makes the achievement of the primary goal easier, keeping your attention and energy on each step by step as you go. This eliminates the possibility of frustration and the abandonment of your goal. It keeps you from pulling the sheets up over your head, overwhelmed by the challenge of the whole enchilada.

Okay now, here we go. See if this little foray works as an example:

Ron's a marathon man. He runs end to end, the Boston, and the others, all 26 miles and 385 yards of the course. (Me—ask my wife—I take my family out zooming for a 26-mile drive in the car and I have to lie down and nap when I get home, I'm that worn.) So cheers to him, but still no great running stride for stride with Bill Rodgers or Frank Shorter. How does he do it?

By not running the whole thing at once he wants you to know. And he is serious. Like most marathon runners, Ron keeps going not by focusing on the goal of the whole course, but by breaking the course down into smaller goals. The next drink station, the next hill, the next corner. Each intermediate goal moving him closer to nailing the overall goal of finishing the race. In his mind he is not running the whole race—he is running one mile 26 times. The 385 yards he tacks on.

Now I don't know about you, but when somebody clues me in to the philosophy behind successfully running 26 miles and 385 yards, before too many hours go by, I'll go along with it.

In other words, there is no sudden leap into success. By dividing your goal into smaller incremental workable goals or steps, you are creating the beginnings of a strategic plan that will allow you to accomplish the achievement of the larger goal. Each step or task you successfully achieve sends an affirmative message to your brain that you possess the motivation, skills, talent and stamina necessary to succeed and triumph.

But dear readers understand—goal setting is just one part of the process of catching and living your dream. Once you have set course on your specific destination—your goal—you next need to carefully chart your points of the compass, your plan. True success and joy are not the result of happenstance and good intention. They evolve into being as outcomes of intelligent planning. So while a goal is likened to a specific destination, a plan is like the rudder of a ship, giving you control of the direction you wish to sail. Absence of a well-thought out, detailed plan would be like sailing without a rudder.

An aimless journey.

Social scientists have found that though most people know what they would like for themselves from life, sadly, the frightener is that only a very *minute* percentage of the population—*less than 3 percent*—has a well-defined plan for obtaining what they want.

Now certainly, logic apparent, this is a grand spot to spend the next bunch of pages getting into the facilitation patterns of what these sociology-meisters recommend in the way of creating and executing an integral and connective modular, self-development plan. Not necessarily a bad thing, but before you go throwing the book across the room, don't worry, we're not going there.

Too complicated to wrap and package.

What we are going to do here is pause to present a no-nonsense, nuts-and-bolts plan to pull you out of the comfort zone of your pit and turn you into a zest-for-life dragon-slayer.

But first you need a clean slate.

Take a quick zip over to your neighborhood office supply and green-light yourself the purchase of a daily planner. A favorite? The Franklin Daily Planner is a popular hands-down choice by most. More than an ordinary date book, it is a dream management tool. Perfect for establishing the power of your personal intent to manifest your life's blueprint. But any notebook will do.

People, understand something: Articulating your goals is the brick-by-brick building of your house of success. By taking this must-do step of sitting down and creating a written plan, through the use of a daily planner, it is more likely that you will do what it takes to actualize the plan and achieve your personal destiny. You will know that every day is a new opportunity.

Begin the process by writing a headline at the top of the page using your goal statement: I am_____. Then every morning as you begin to plan your day, take a moment to look at what you've written and visualize yourself as the headline states. Know that you are deserving of the success it proclaims. Believe in the power of your purpose.

Believe in yourself.

Positive self-esteem is the foundation for success. And as a successful person it is your personal responsibility to *reaffirm* your commitment to your commitment. Take a solemn oath to spend thirty seconds, each morning, to repledge to yourself to become the person you want to become. Secure a supreme confidence in yourself and in your abilities to achieve what you want to accomplish. With a passionate determination to succeed you will not be defeated. Life *will* change. You *will* fulfill the vision of your new self.

Next, list the changes essential to reach your headline goal statement. Identify the support steps required to actualize it and slave to get it right. As skillfully and scrupulously as you can, write down the experience and acquisition of knowledge you will need. Determine what help, assistance or resources you will have to knit together. Be precise in knowing what, why, when and how you will administer the techniques necessary to unfold your soul's intent and achieve your future.

Think about it.

Then think about taking great care in developing a plan in which you have as much control as possible. The more your plan is based on your own personal performance, the more likely it is that you will do what it takes to follow through, day to day. There is nothing more disheartening than stalling, or worse, failing to achieve a personal goal due to the dependence on—or the nonsuccess of—others. Possessing the power to move your plan forward, you are able to activate your natural vitality, compassion and personal intent and shout up to the gods that you can control your destiny and weave a life from your heart's deepest aspirations.

And because it's always something and shit happens—yes? And no plan is really bulletproof, it's important to consider all possible obstacles and have a strategy for dealing with them. Conceive contingency plans.

Do not let the unexpected act on you.

Act on the unexpected.

You must possess the flexibility and the acuity to create new success strategies and plans to take the place of those that have failed. The purpose of launching a plan is to offer a clear-cut picture of what you have to do to overcome and reach your goal and to protect yourself from being a powerless victim of circumstances. Still, the landscape will change, and unforeseen circumstances may appear on your horizon. When this occurs, sense what is in the air, alter your course and modify or change your approach.

Most importantly, develop and write down a series of action steps that will execute your plan and connect each step of the way with a timetable of daily, weekly or monthly target dates for accomplishing each phase. Be specific and definitive. One of the great truths is: *deadlines stimulate action*. More than anything else, action must be taken without fail, each and every day, toward clocking some incremental progress toward achieving your goal. An ancient Sanskrit proverb states: *Today well lived makes every tomorrow closer to hope.* No matter how bullshitty your day is going, you must take at the very least, some forward action. Sit and reflect about your goal, write down one new idea, listen to a motivational tape, read an article or some pages of a book regarding your desire. Rent a biographical video of people who have overcome circumstance to become successful, talk to some knowledgeable friends, counselors, associates. Sit in front of a computer and surf the turf learning all you can about electronic networking. Do something that furthers your progress toward taking another step and another.

To repeat, success is a step-by-step process. So use your daily planner to evaluate your headway. Remember that inking deadline dates means nothing if you do not take the time to monitor and review your strategy. Take stock of what is working and what isn't. If certain action steps are not working, then don't waste any more time with them. Cut loose, disco them, refigure and move on.

Most importantly, each day, each night, each whatever, schedule time for yourself, your relationships, your relaxation—carve some time in your day planner for caring for yourself, physically, mentally, emotionally and spiritually. Don't let the simplest pleasures of everyday life slip away. Take time to sensitize yourself to the fundamental beauty of life that surrounds you. The sermons of a bird. The freshness of a breeze. The flowers of the season. The unfolding splendor of a sunrise, a sunset. Keep the time you spend on yourself sacred. A thousand years ago and more, a Chinese Zen master wrote: *Magical power, marvelous action. Chop wood. Carry water.* This most ancient and most contemporary message speaks to the purpose of our existence—that the greatest joy and the profoundest contentment of our journey path can be found in our presence of being, the paying of care and attention we give to each and every moment in our everyday life. Have a full awareness, pay a refined alacrity to the things you do and make, your essential existence; celebrate and enjoy the daily events that are the marvel of life. Forget about the *then* and *there*. Your life is happening *here* and *now*. Before enlightenment, chop wood, carry water. After enlightenment, chop wood, carry water. The actions may appear to be the same, but the motivation makes all the difference. Devote attention to living with a conscious mindfulness in your daily reality. Be sublime about such moments.

And then, and this is crucial: Dive into the mosh pit and raise the roof.

Have some big kid fun. Pop a cork and enjoy the satisfaction of your achievements. You deserve it. The good Dr. Seuss said it best: *If you never did, you should. These things are fun and fun is good.*

By celebrating your successes you will glean gratification and joy from your accomplishments, providing your internal government with the confidence and self-assurance to attain higher and more difficult goals. Never deprive yourself of the pleasure of your achievements. Realize that you did it because you could! Every victory toward your goal—no matter how small—is a milepost along the dream-seeking trail and should be documented in your daily planner and celebrated.

Successful people feed on progress. At day's end, instead of dwelling on the difficulties and the undone, end each day with a positive note, jotting down a good thing that happened. When you find yourself in a crunch, feeling discouraged or having doubts, your record of past successes will give you the encouragement and self-propelling power to bounce back.

Nutshelling it: when you articulate your plans and goals on paper, you are putting both your conscious and subconscious on record, stating that you will not allow frustration, discouragement or circumstances to prevent you from living the dream you desire and deserve. By taking the time each and every day to consult your planner, you will put purpose and direction into your daily actions and realize the success and unlimited power that comes from . . .

Doing the write thing.

The natural way is the way.
Those who know the journey path
know the way to yield.
To yield is to become.
Only then will the true way
of the Universe be observed.
For it is the way.

SHI BAI

Chapter Six

ON YOUR MARK...
GET SET...

FAIL

Fall seven times,

stand up eight.

—*Ancient Chinese proverb*

Okay, kiddos, here's the kicker.

Moved by these pages you are ready to put into practice what we've preached. You're psyched, stoked, ready to throw down, empowered fully and completely with the excitement that your life is *clearly going to change*. Because you've discovered your passion, know your life's purpose, embrace who you are and understand absolutely *what* you are—without question—capable of. Full of motivation and razor-sharp focus, you've made an unrelenting and steadfast commitment to your goals and to your dream. Delivering yourself from the emotional frenzy and chaos of a once uncertain self, you sought and found a mentor who has illuminated your spirit, provided you with wisdom and guidance and has inspired you to greater achievement. Because of all this and more, no one will ever know how hard you slaved to get to the point that allows you—now—to draw on the confidence of your strengths and skills, your unique combination of talent and mind and emotional courage to understand and accept the challenges of risk. And on and on you go, standing rock solid, ready with the knowledge and insight, the earnestness and courage to do all that is necessary to succeed at life and catch and live your dream, and if you said "YESS!" to all our cogent comments and followed the criterion given, and if you know down deep in your soul that the course you will take is as right as right could possibly be. . . . Guess what?

You're going to fail.

And that's being optimistic.

Because chances are you're going to fail miserably. It's as simple and as discouraging as that.

And you will be shocked and saddened, embarrassed, maybe even humiliated, certainly pissed. The blinding awfulness of your failure will be like a knife in the heart, leaving you mentally and physically reeling— a fish-flopping gasping-for-air emotional wreck. And if you get the sense that this would be as good a place as any to offer up a suggestion of some sort of a silver lining, you are correct. And here it is: as devastating as failure is, there is something much more tragic and terribly worse—the absence of failure.

If there is no failure it's because there has been no attempt.

And that, class, would be the most egregious failure of all.

Because not to risk failure is not to risk success.

Thomas Edison had almost ten thousand unsuccessful attempts before he invented and perfected the incandescent lamp. Talk about seeing only darkness and failure! However, when asked by a reporter if he would continue to fail, Edison said, "I haven't even failed once. Nine thousand times I've learned what doesn't work."

~ 104 ~

And if a lightbulb just went on over your head, then you do indeed now see the light. Successful people understand that failure is not final, but rather it is an important step to learn and prepare for the next step to success.

Not that we're suggesting it's plenty okay to go around telling all who will listen, "I just can't wait to fail again." That kind of talk will get you a good 42nd Street corner on which to squeegee windshields from. What is being presented here is the fact that successful people possess a pit-bull, dogged determination to learn from their failures and move on to try again.

And again.

Because failure is the lubricant of success. As shitty and as paralyzingly painful as failure may be, it is an essential building block needed to succeed. And how you handle failure is the single hardest battle you must face in accomplishing your dream.

Get behind this: successful people don't dwell on failure and will not allow their failure to stand in their path to success. They turn the blink of failure into a long and hard stare of opportunity. They work through it, learn from the experience, minimize its negative impact, grow, and then dismiss it from their mind, moving on with new spirit, energy and resolve. And since you are going to be successful, you too must do the same.

Adopt a philosophy and a belief that there is no such thing as failure, that each and every setback is an opportunity to grow personally and professionally, a learning experience that will provide you with the wisdom, insight and knowledge to overcome obstacles, reach your goals, and achieve your dream.

The Chinese write the word *impasse* in two characters—one meaning danger and the other meaning opportunity. How wise. With every failure there is the danger of being defeated or the opportunity for growth.

With this in mind, the following needs a bit of pausing over—not because of the nifty advice that it fiddles to forward—but as permanent and meaningful lessons to take to heart. Let's just call the next four paragraphs a quick enrollment into a failure **GRAD** program, here at Ron and Stuart's *University of Adversity*. Sixty secs from now and you'll possess a Master's Degree in overcoming the crisis of failure.

Get over it. Realize that all you did was fail. It happens to everyone along the dream-seeking trail. It's how we as intelligent human beings learn and grow into the roles we were meant to play. Don't dwell on it. Understand why and how you failed and move on. If you learn from the failure, you need never again repeat it. Know that failure is an important step to learn and to prepare for the next step to success. Ancient Chinese proverb: *Fall seven times, stand up eight.* Our translation: success stops when you do.

Redefine your failure. Adjust your thinking to appreciate that failure leads to success. Failure teaches you very clearly and precisely *what not to do*. Make enough mistakes and the end result will be that you will know precisely what to do. Thomas Watson, founder of IBM, said, "If you want to double your success rate you have to double your failure rate." Again, realize that every failure is a chance for growth.

Analyze failure. Study what you did wrong and march on through it. Use the experience to evaluate your results objectively, to understand yourself better and to get some perspective on your life. What new attitudes and skills must you gain to create a different outcome next time? Take control. Look at failure as an opportunity to review, revise, regroup and replan.

Depersonalize your failure. Get off your back. Understand that failure is a part of the human experience. It's normal to fail. It is part of the divine plan for success. To find a strategy that works, you must go through several strategies that don't. For every great achievement, there are several attempts. Some of the greatest successes are the result of the failure of an initial idea.

So the real question is not whether you will fail, but rather *how will you handle it* when you do? Will you cave, lose sight of your vision, give in to the word *impossible?* Or will you keep a positive, passionate, focused mind and use your failure as a ticket to begin again?

Will you use the experience to learn, renew and to grow?

Note:

On May 29, 1953, Sir Edmund Hillary was the first human to climb the twenty-nine thousand straight-up feet of Mount Everest. But before this success there was his failed attempt at scaling this same greatness many months before. After his failure, in front of a hall full of well-wishers he was asked if he would ever try again. Moving away from the podium and turning to face the picture of Everest behind him, Hillary shook a defiant fist at the mountain. "Mount Everest, you beat me this time, but I'll beat you the next time because you've grown all you are going to grow. But I'm still growing!"

And so it is, most look up and admire the stars. A success climbs a mountain and grabs one.

Without the remotest exception, there is no single fact of more import than the self-realization that you and you alone have the power to live your dream. You have the courage and strength, the personal muscle, to reach down deep within your heart and soul and draw up the indomitable spirit needed to persevere. And persevere you must. Never, ever give in to the obstacles and setbacks that will be thrown your way. Every minute of every hour of every day is yours to live with passion and purpose, to go after and succeed. You can and you will overcome and triumph. You must keep the faith in yourself, and keep focusing on your wishes, goals, desires and dreams, because you are deserving and have the potential and the power to make them come true. Once you have determined your life's mission, let no failure keep you from your goal. Stay compelled and committed, cutting off all other possibilities. Never, never, *never* give up on your dream!

Never!

The editors of *Time* magazine and CBS News recently compiled a selection of this past century's one hundred most influential people—people who have left an indelible mark and legacy on our world. The list is part of a book titled *People of the Century: One Hundred Men and Women Who Shaped the Last One Hundred Years*. The book's foreword is written by Dan Rather. When the legendary news anchor was asked who he thought should appear at the very top, he was quick to give his answer: Winston Churchill. When asked why, this eyewitness to decades of history was even quicker to reply, explaining that in the face of overwhelming odds and certain defeat, Sir Winston Churchill did much to change the course of human history with little more than the following two brief sentences:

"Never give up! Never, never give up."

Now no one can say with any authoritative precision who should indeed occupy the top of such a prestigious and humbling list, but there is one thing I bet all could fully agree on, for sure, and it is this . . .

Such are the words of greatness.

ENSO

Chapter Seven
ON BEING A
ZENTREPRENEUR

ACT YOUR
SAGE

Tell me, I'll forget. Show me, I may remember.

But involve me and I'll understand.

—Chinese Proverb

Inside out.

That is what you must know if you want to more fully grasp the connective kernels that can marvelously incarnate you into the Zentrepreneur's way of life.

In other words, to achieve enlightenment and the ultimate reality of a true Zentrepreneur, you must journey toward an inner understanding of self and life, creating new ways of knowing and doing as your path emerges to the outside world. Of course, there is other stuff to know, sure, but nothing can be more difficult—or easier—than the first step. So as a teaching tool here, it would be useful to describe one of the most frequently occurring designs in Zen brushed-ink paintings, the *enso*.

The enso is a simple circle created when a Zen monk, while meditating on the emptiness of blank rice paper, takes up a large sumi brush full of black ink. Upon reaching unobstructed fluidity, the monk spontaneously throws all of himself into a moment's swift action of painting—with a single brush stroke—the perfect circle. Not mathematically correct, mind you, where every point in the circle is of equal distance from the center; but nevertheless, it is the manifestation of perfection, still, because of the way in which it wondrously reveals the concentrated thought and pure energy of the artisan. It is understood that when the Zen master brushes an enso, he is expressing a dramatic conveyance of power and emotion which allows the mind and spirit to act, do and create. His very life force and enlightenment are imparted to the ink and to the paper. Both internally and externally.

Inside out.

And do not doubt the significance of what this simple brushed circle has represented over the course of centuries. The circle shape of the enso symbolizes a myriad of deeply held spiritual and philosophical ideas. It is a symbol of simplicity and profundity. It represents the true nature of reality and enlightenment. The circle of all things seen and unseen. The circle of endings and of beginnings. The circle of balance and harmony. The circle of what the *Tao Te Ching* refers to as the *Ten Thousand Things*. To enter and dissolve into the enso is to surrender to your true self, to your unique gifts and abilities, to merge with the circle of life. To do what you were born to do.

Dharma.

Now we don't want this to come off as New-Age mystical mumbo. It isn't. Dharma is the inherent way all things are intended to be. It means working in accord with your own true nature, embracing your life's calling, striving for your greater heart. Striking a balance and harmony between your inborn gifts and your outward expression of them. Like the creative force behind the enso, a Zentrepreneur releases the powerful force within, creating forms of splendor in all he or she attempts. By applying mind, body and spirit to any endeavor or creation, by expressing their inmost nature to the outside world, the Zentrepeneur becomes a living art form. A true masterwork in progress.

Again: inside out.

And that is but one of the important patterns woven into the life fabric of a Zentrepreneur. In our unceasing pursuit of truth-telling and accuracy, here are a few more:

Zentrepreneurs have unconditional self-regard. Trusting his or her own instincts, they spend little or no time thinking about what they can't do and instead think entirely in terms of what they *can* and *must* do to catch and live their dreams.

A Zentrepreneur exercises joy and sincerity, promotes illumination, and actively seeks inspiration and gives inspiration to others. He or she shares wisdom, moving toward ever-greater harmony and balance, energizing others with their own enthusiasm.

Zentrepreneurs enchant their lives with confidence and hope, realizing that they have the energy to cope with circumstances, and that they also possess the power to generate new possibilities of thought and action.

Zentrepeneurs deal with events directly and clearly,

managing their minds with flexibility and managing their bodies with calmness.

A Zentrepreneur gravitates towards positive people and situations, seeking out those who will support and inspire, cutting away from those who discourage, distract or undermine.

A Zentrepreneur knows that to move on, sometimes the best light for the journey can be the result of a burning bridge.

Zentrepreneurs are spiritual human beings making time to celebrate the beauty and the mystery of life. They recognize the creative intelligence of the universe and respect the interdependent synchronicity of all things. If a butterfly flaps its wings in Japan, a breeze can be felt in the Caribbean. Everything is connected. The nineteenth-century naturalist John Muir said, "When we tug at a single thing in nature we find that it is attached to the rest of the world." Zentrepreneurs embrace the process of life, allowing themselves to be taken with the spiritual energies of the universe, knowing that they too are part of the unity of all things.

A Zentrepreneur recognizes that the process of attaining success at life is filled with disappointment, rejection, frustration, failure, stress, sacrifice and loneliness. And so what. A true Zentrepreneur also knows that these things happen because life happens, and life is an ongoing dialogue with change. And change for a Zentrepreneur, like the beauty of a flower, is ordinary activity.

Not a bad sampling to hold on to, and for the uninitiated, we would like to proffer one more verrry important touchstone, and that is:

Zentrepreneurs value their humanity and strive to be spirits of compassion, giving of themselves freely and without hesitation. They appreciate that the most exalted service is to help and to seek the welfare of others, without expectation of reward. The *Tao Te Ching* declares that the way of selfless service is the fundamental principle that sustains the universe: *By placing himself in the background, the sage finds himself in the foreground.* Translation: what goes around comes around. Since all things are interconnected, nothing we do is self-contained. Everything we do generates a nexus of energy that flows out into the world and eventually returns to the source. Giving of your wisdom, value and service to others is like casting a pebble into the water. After the brevity of its drop, the ripples of energy continue to extend endlessly outward and in due course return to the Zentrepreneur's heart and soul manyfold. Again, everything is connected.

And so now, fellow troopers, if there is one lesson we want you to learn in our little career camp today, that is it. Honor yourself and others with a life of full-heartedness. Practice the highest form of service, that of selfless service, engaging in motiveless granting of your gifts, your talents, your abundance of material prosperity. Give something of yourself to others without any expectation other than the personal satisfaction of knowing that you have helped somebody, somewhere along the way.

At The Republic of Tea we hold this philosophy in high reverence. In our little Republic we support and donate our time and treasury to many worthwhile and deserving causes, dedicating a portion of ourselves to the force for positive change. One of our honors has been to create SIP FOR THE CURE TEAS, extolling the work of The Susan G. Komen Foundation, known for their Race For The Cure events and credited as the nation's leading catalyst in the fight to eradicate breast cancer. We also donate a portion of the proceeds from the sale of our popular RAINFOREST TEA directly to the Sierra Santa Marta Project, a nonprofit group that helps villagers develop sustainable economics compatible with rainforest preservation. And profoundly dear to our hearts is our KID'S CUPPA program, where we allocate a portion of the sales of this special tea to support The Sunny Hills Children's Garden and their programs and treatments for abused and neglected children. Remember, please, by helping others, we help ourselves.

Again:

Everything is connected. As citizens of the world we are one with everything, experiencing ourselves as one with all of life. To have the desire to make a difference in the lives of others is to make yourself fully alive. By helping to change other people's lives, ours change too. And please believe that we can go on and on about the true bliss that selfless service brings to all of us who are part of The Republic of Tea, but to put a finer point on it: each night we all snore with happiness.

In charting your path to success at life, it is our hope that you will embrace and integrate these Zentrepreneurial traits of wholeness and consciousness into new ways of thinking, feeling, seeing and doing. Everyone possesses the inner treasures of a Zentrepreneur. Most people lack awareness, more than most never bother to seek the inner profoundness of the treasures they possess. Here again, it is the practice of mindfulness that can make one a sage. There is an ancient Zen koan about two men staring up, watching the sway of a tree branch. "It is the wind that is moving," said one. "It is the branch that is moving," said the other. A Zen Master overhearing the discussion admonished them both: "It is the mind that moves." Without changing anything else, if you change your attitude, you can change everything else. Indeed, you can change the world.

Not too long ago, Ron and I had the pleasure of addressing a lively organization of young, well-to-do brighteners—over a hundred or so MBA's, entrepreneurs, marketers and investors—all sardined into one room, sharing the delight and enthusiasm that comes with following one's dream. And it was almost frightening how successful and financially well-off some of these youngins already were. Not surprising, mind you, because these were people who were committed to pushing the world forward, persisting in their passions, pursuing positive possibilities, all of them confident that they have what it takes to make success their constant companion. Truly they did.

Anyway, there Ron and I were, doing what we were graciously invited to do, addressing their questions about business and life, offering with humility our thoughts and philosophies on how to further their way. And at first the seminar started off like most sort of do—studiously—everyone politely listening. Then the questions came: What's the best way to do this? How do you go about doing that? And all of the dialogue mattered, everyone taking part in the back and forth, one question becoming the source of inspiration for another. It didn't take long for everything to kick into higher gear, the room spinning with the energy of people who sincerely seek to make a real difference.

And what better place for magic than a roomful of young driven dynamos? All determined and smart as hell, no chickenshits here, these were rebels without a pause, intent on running full out to catch and live their dreams. Clever, able and confident that they too could be called Zentrepreneurs, because as I said, most had already accomplished great things; many had already accumulated great abundance, but before too much time escaped, I had to ask a question of lasting import: What things had they done to benefit the welfare of others, what selfless service had they given to help shine their fellow beings?

The question washed over all the listeners as Ron and I stood at the podium and waited.

And waited.

And waited some more, while, sadly, no one in the room raised a hand.

MI

Chapter Eight
SECRETS OF THE TEMPLE

FOR NOW
AND ZEN

When an old pond gets a new frog,

it's a new pond.

—*Ancient Japanese poem*

There are many great truths to be gathered out there along the dream-seeking trail and one of them is absolutely this:

Regis wants to give away the million.

And unless you have just come down from many months of stick-walking the Himalayas, or have spent the better part of your time in the botanical back bush of the Brazilian rain forest, you know that we are referring to the bodacious spectacle of Regis Philbin's mega-hit game show *Who Wants to Be a Millionaire*.

In this prime-timer quiz spectacle they sure didn't underestimate the dumbness of the viewing public, offering contestants from across America the chance to become instant millionaires by answering such brainiac questions as: Which U.S. President made a guest appearance on TV's *Laugh In*? (Nixon, the laughably easy answer for most adults, was the clincher that won the first million.)

Still, even the dimmest bulbs can become bright and win a ton with the offered multiple-choice options and the allowed on-air phone calls to friends and family for help with the answers.

And as we sit here now pounding out these pages, at

this moment, the show is already big and still building—and who can know how long the craze of the thing
will last? But one thing that you can know is this: As
long as the ratings are a sweep and the masses keep
watching, ABC will keep writing out the checks allowing the gregarious Regis to happily anoint another millionaire.

Now if you're wondering where we're going with
this, there is a reason for stepping off the curb here, I
swear, and we will get to it in just a sec.

After we invite you to play a sample round of this
gamey show.

Of course, as stated, we are trying to take this somewhere, hence to reach our segue, we want to warn you
upfront that the question will require some dollop of intelligence. Here goes.

For a million bucks . . .

The United States Army has asked for and received
approval for which of the following?

Is it . . .

A) A new generation of Apache attack helicopters

B) Better living and pay standards

C) Yoga lessons

D) A faster M1 tank

Hmmm. . . .

We're talking a million scoots, so take a second and
think real hard. There's no lock here. No easy answer.
Even Regis would be taking a peek at his screen. Got
your pick?

Confident?

Final answer?

If you picked "A," the Apache attack helicopters—in my opinion, a splendid choice—I wouldn't blame you a bit.

But you are wrong!

And personally I wouldn't find fault with your pick of "B," if that's where you went. Because I too think that our men and women who serve deserve better housing and pay for keeping the demons at bay. However, if "B" was your choice, your heart was in the right place but your choice wasn't.

You still lose!

And while we're at it, if "D" was what you hung your hat on—forget about it. You're hosed.

But if by some stunning miracle you chose "C," then back up the Brinks truck. You win!

Hard to believe, I know. But as we enter the twenty-first century, the U.S. Army, the same army that is having trouble accepting women and that maintains the don't ask–don't tell policy, has embraced the *om's* of yoga as part of their drills.

Kidding? Nope.

In a policy decision of breathtaking surprise, the army powers-that-be have come to the realization that enlightenment is not just for the sages. The upper brass wants GIs of the new millennium to learn to align their bodies and minds based on the belief that through the ancient philosophy of yoga or Pilates, soldiers can be empowered to brave life's adventures and assaults.

Can you believe it?

Now if the news of America's army accepting yoga as a means of mastering the commonplace has gotten your attention, we are ready to reconvene and set up shop, and discuss one of the most important *successories* you must own in order to achieve a capacity to cope with life's circumstances and fulfill the destiny of your dream.

Being a Master.

No exotic or faraway mystical mumbo jumbo, know that within us all, we possess a unique essence—a self-enhancing actualizing power—to master our own destiny. Whatever your psychology or physiology—your age, your sex, your race, your socio-economic upbringing or education—the true fact of the matter without exception is that what you *really* are, mostly, at this very moment, is untapped potential.

Listen, we touched on this before and it's important enough to reach out for it again. The mastering, the self-actualization of your talents, capacities and potentialities are an integral part of the cosmos—your evolutionary destiny. The purpose of your life is to harness the power inside yourself so that your deeper self may guide you to the reality within you. By discovering your true center you will gain a life of success, satisfaction and serenity.

However, in order to walk the path of mastery and enable yourself to respond to all of life's challenges and opportunities, and to empower yourself to live your dream, you must possess the power of a Master. You must be able to attain enlightenment, and tune in to an inner state of strength and personal tranquility that will allow you to unleash your potential and call upon and take full advantage of your unique talents and gifts.

To use what is unused.

But to be a Master, you have to *become* a Master. And for that you have to know the *way*.

Not to go soapbox Zen on you, but by using the word *way*, what we are invoking is the spiritual dimension of the Chinese word *Tao* and the Japanese word *do*, both of which mean path or way—a holistic, transcendent concept. Interpreted not as a road or trail, but as a dynamic—a method, principle, or doctrine, which when practiced results in perfecting one's higher self, physically, mentally and spiritually.

To become enlightened is to gather teeming energy through the discovery of a life of health, balance and well-being, which leads us to grow *beyond* ourselves *to* ourselves—to journey upward to our highest level of consciousness, and through mind and body, rise above the forces, opinions, conceits and falsehoods that can confront and exert a discouraging and negative influence over our life theme. By achieving this inner unity, sense and essence merge. We discover our beginner's mind, an origin of ultimate reality, which allows us intuitive wisdom, rather than the entanglements of rational knowledge. This awareness activates our *chi*, the life force of vitality, energy and spirit. This unification of mind, body and will can empower us to be true to our life purpose, the spark of the divine that speaks to our heart and gives us our true nature.

And lets us fly.

Now if this sounds like Buddha chic to the uninitiated, we understand, what with the pretentious plethora of Zen merchandising showing up throughout the malls and on the shelves of big name retailers. And since America has gone star crazy maybe it's watching and listening to Madonna trying to get much cleverer by offering a world of wonder on her Grammy-winning *Ray of Light* album. Or watching other style-conscious celebheads like Courtney Love, Natalie Merchant, Sonic Youth, Foo Fighters, Beastie Boys and Porno for Pyros, who have attached themselves to the jiffy Zen trend—as long as it's free of the baggage of a lifetime commitment. A kind of Buddha unleaded. And for us Woodstockers, there's Steven Seagal, Tina Turner and Herbie Hancock, just a few of the wizened elders demonstrating John Lennon's admonition that "Instant karma's gonna get you." Not a big TV *Dharma and Greg* fan? Switch channels and there's more kharma clatter with Larry King interviewing the Dalai Lama, the exiled spiritual leader of the Tibetan people. Missed it? Bop on over to Blockbuster and rent the life story of his great and good heart in the bioflix *Kundun* from Martin Scorsese or *Seven Years in Tibet*, starring Brad Pitt. And just for good measure type in Zen on **www.Amazon.com,** and a harder to dismiss listing of over 1,669 titles should convince even the most ardent Richard Gere hater that there must be something to this Buddha blizzard.

Which, after all, there is.

Albert Einstein, who was only smarter than all of us, said, "You cannot solve a problem with the same consciousness that created it." To underscore, a recent study of Fortune 500 CEO's found that these successful people relied upon set-aside periods in their daily schedules for quiet reflection. The sheer busyness of business requires, demands, this need for a clear space. They reported that some sort of centering meditative exercise was essential for them to reconnect with their intuition and inspiration, allowing them to think clearly and insightfully, helping them to make more effective decisions. Chuang Tzu noted that when people wish to see their reflections, they do not look into running water, they look into still water. By allocating time with themselves *for* themselves, they are able to achieve a personal transcendence that nourishes and exercises mental and spiritual well-being. This effecting of both an outer and an inner fitness has helped them to find the wisdom of the real bottom line:

A healthy mind and body is the true incontestable currency of success.

Now there is a lesson to be learned through this example, actually two. The first is, that one great piece of advice is something we should all be grateful for. And the second: In order to become a success at life and live your dream, understand that you must take care of your gifts.

Pleeease take care of your gifts.

Like successful CEO's, successful business owners,

professionals and entrepreneurs all have one important trait in common—a remarkable inexhaustible source of Self. They are able to tap a wonderful positive mental energy and stamina that lurks within, providing knowledge, insight and a positive motivation for themselves, empowering their clear sense of purpose. They know how to strike a chord that resonates with their true talents and gifts, allowing the body, mind and spirit to rise above defeatist patterns and engage life to the fullest. In other words:

They've got game.

They jog, swim, bike, hike, roller blade, play racquet-ball, jazzercise, work out at the gym—some sort of regular exercise that frees their minds from mental gravity, reduces their stress, increases their energy, and turbo-charges their tenacity and perseverance. Despite their interests and lifestyles being clearly spread, they all have recognized the importance of how a higher awareness of mental, physical, emotional and spiritual mastery is essential to powering the processes that manifest their destiny. Buddha said, "To keep the body in good health is a duty. Otherwise we shall not be able to keep our mind strong and clear."

So, again, take care of your gifts.

Become a Zentrepreneur by finding joy and appreciation in the wonder of your lifetime, by embracing harmony, vitality and well-being in your daily life. Go from filling the hole to *becoming* whole, evoking and nurturing your center—your Essential Self. Recognize there is nothing elusive about the union of mind and body. Know that encoded deeply within your organic being, true health and happiness are there for you, if you are there for them.

Important note. Before we go any further, be sure to consult your physician before taking on any new exercise program. As Han Solo remarked a long time ago in a galaxy far, far way: "What good's a reward if you ain't around to use it?" So chat it up with your sawbones and get their advice. Then yabba dabba do it!

Many recent studies show that to cut your risk of heart disease, control your weight and achieve mental energy and vibrancy, you should start a program of daily physical activity that will elevate your heart rate for a good thirty minutes. You'll gleefully notice a difference shortly after you begin, as your lungs fill your brain with creativity-generating oxygen and stimulating inspiration. Your blood pressure will lower, your cholesterol levels will improve. You will begin to possess a "beingness" that will allow you to seize the wondrous opportunities and sunny pleasures that lie ahead.

But wait, this does not mean you have to grind yourself as if you were training for a triathlon. If perfect arms or legs that run forever have you panicked, there is a whole bushel of stuff you can do. Be realistic, figure a fitness program with an activity you enjoy. That way you're more likely to stick with it—do it more often. Hopefully, it will become a routine. Turn on the tube and watch fitness shows and follow along, buy a video, try a sport. The fact is, any regular exercise will reduce stress, increase your energy and make you alert, confident and fortified. Even a daily walk at a pace just fast enough to speed up your breathing a bit will improve your overall fitness.

Now, personally, having no desire to grace the cover of the next issue of *Muscle Fitness*, I choose to enjoy the quietude of a daily mile or more stroll. I live a spit away from the ocean, and find that a walk or two a day for me is not only a way of increasing physical activity, but also results in an ability to more easily achieve a higher level of productivity. Going out for a simple walk brings about a sense of peace, rejuvenation, a restoration of true health and an inner happiness—a wonder and exuberance for all life has to offer. It didn't take long for me to discover that by going out, I was really going *in*. Feeling everything around me and in me. Balancing body and mind through quiet reflection, I become testimony to a radiant sense of power.

And believe it, you don't need a gate to the breakers to keep you relatively fit and balanced, folks. Wherever your crib, a brisk go-go walk around in the fresh air will offer the opportunity to see into the truth of your life, permitting you to generate new possibilities of thought and action. Oliver Wendell Holmes said, "A mind once expanded by a new idea never returns to its original dimension." How simple. The marvelous pleasure of connecting with your true self, listening to the goodness of your inner voice, will allow you to seek inspiration, daydream, brainstorm and plan your day—tacking on the bonus of empowering your body at the same time.

And since our bodies are the instruments by which we carry out our actions, when hunger comes calling, we urge you not to dig your grave with your own knife and fork and, instead, follow the mystical drumbeat of good nutrition. Chances are you know the drill concerning a healthy diet. No need to McMess around, other than to emphasize with utmost import that the worlds of sound nutrition and personal success move through each other. You cannot possess the energy and stamina needed to catch and live your dream without regard for the alliance between a healthy diet and a fit life.

And for the few lost souls who actually believe that a Grand Slam breakfast is the fuel to stoke the fire of success, we fault you not. Our public education system is sooo lacking in providing the proper nutritional guidelines necessary for the attainment of self-mastery and the fostering of well-being that it's a damn shame. Sadder still is the bombardment of diet books and how-to books on health which in general proffer little more than stupendously uninteresting nutritional nuggets from contented celebrity *du jours*.

Puh-leeeze.

Look, each of us makes dozens of dietary decisions a day but most of us are lacking a culinary consciousness with respect to what foods furnish us with the type of optimizing health and vigor that is necessary to control our fates. Doctors now agree that ninety percent of sickness and disease is connected to a faulty diet, which is why we would like to include this plea:

Get a shelf life.

Troop over to your neighborhood bookseller and check out the selection of books that will ready you with the teachings and techniques that will help you create a wellness menu for success. Avoid the latest fad diets, realizing that they are just that, fad diets, sans the details of sound, validated views. Search out those titles that go beyond the everyday advice that veggies are good for you, in favor of a personalized approach based on your unique individual variation.

We tell you this (and it can't be overemphasized enough) to let you know that you are a one-of-a-kind special. And never forget that. You, we, he, she—all of us—are. Each with our own metabolic and genetic balancing needs. Recognizing this, research today is discovering that certain nutritional facts do not necessarily apply to all types. The old adage about one man's food being another man's poison is now the subject of much important study, leading more and more people to the concept of individualized nutrition. We recommend that you take the time to explore and examine this new terrain of persuasive findings, some of which are currently presented in several best-selling books.

Eat Right 4 Your Type, by Dr. Peter J. D'Adamo, is one such offering. Peter is a friend but believe this, does he ever *not* need us pitching him any freebie play here.

For years his *New York Times* best-seller has been going like hotcakes, with no sign of slowing down any time soon. Still, we want to add our voice to its honored praise, in hopes that at the very least, we can urge you to give this remarkable book a solid thumb-through. Another well touted primer is *The Body Code: A Personalized Wellness and Weight Loss Plan Developed at the World Famous Green Valley Spa,* by Jay Cooper.

Consensus: A study of either of these breakthrough books may very well rock your world, and make all the difference in your dream for success.

And while you're already at it, track down books about the benefits of aromatherapy and the ancient Chinese art of Feng Shui. This is not brute work so read, read, read. East has met West, and there's a wealth of material out there about these health and balance practices for life, most of which were not available even a generation ago. And before you go glib and skip right over what we're suggesting, know that I too remember the moment these practices were first told to me. I listened to the strange explanation as it went on and on and pretended to be interested, all the while looking at this person and thinking to myself: Some poor village is short their idiot.

But that was way before I knew of their pedigrees.

With a history thousands of years long, aromatherapy and Feng Shui are part of the fabric of life of many cultures. Plus now, recent studies here and in Europe are extolling the benefits of the psychological ergonomics of Feng Shui, and the mind-body medicinal benefits of aromatherapy.

Considerable evidence now exists that the inhalation of certain fragrant compounds and essential oils can alleviate stress and fatigue, abate pain, and invigorate the entire body. Researchers in England found that some scents, such as lavender and rosemary, increase alpha brain waves associated with relaxation, and they are using it instead of medication to relieve insomnia. Jasmine and eucalyptus, on the other hand, have been found to be uplifting fragrances that increase beta waves linked to a more alert state.

This awakening to the healing and mood enhancement benefits of aromatherapy in western culture is propelling it to one of the fastest growing fields in alternative medicine. To decrease your mental tension or to boost your mental energy, for emotional and physical health and harmonal well-being, try it—tap into the empowerment of aromatherapy. Discover the way of the earth's wisdom, and you will discover the *way*.

Now, about Feng Shui. For centuries, ancient cultures were adept at recognizing the subtle invisible living energy of *Chi*, using it for auspicious results. This balancing and harmonizing of the earth's dynamic energy is thought to have something to do with the riddle of Stonehenge, and with the Egyptian and Mayan placement of the pyramids. Europeans practice the art and purpose of placement, calling it geomancy. Native Americans have always respected the patterns of nature, ensuring that beneficial energy flows within and around their environment. And now the rest of the West is catching up.

The art and craft of Feng Shui (pronounced "Fung Schway") is a four-thousand-year-old Chinese philosophy that concerns the unimpeded flow of the earth's natural energy—*Chi*—and its relationship with humans and their environment. The words *Feng Shui* literally mean "wind" and "water," representing the ancient Chinese concept of man harmonizing with his environment, bringing about balance in all things seen and unseen. Feng Shui balances the life energies, or *Chi*, in a living space by increasing the flow of positive *Chi* and subduing the negative flow, thereby harmonizing our personal *Chi*—our spirit, our emotions, our subconscious, our creative intellect—with the *Chi* of nature, which is believed to result in a healthy, happy and more prosperous life.

The tenets of this philosophy of environmental balance—that everything around us has the potential to affect our well-being—are gaining increasing acceptance in, of all places, corporate America. Architects and interior designers are employing the Feng Shui principles of proper circulation of energy to everything, from the colors of walls and flooring to the use of metals, woods and plantings, in order to improve productivity, creativity and interpersonal relations. To put a fine point on it, Donald Trump's newest skyscraper is built based on Feng Shui principles. To put a finer point on it still, we of The Republic of Tea have taken great care to create our fifty-thousand square feet of offices and facilities with the belief that by applying Feng Shui, we have created an interactive synergy that will take care of us. By harnessing supportive *Chi* through design, placement, element and color, we believe that Feng Shui creates an ideal, harmonious and balanced environment in which to work, improving the lives of our associates and therefore maximizing the potential for a more joyful and successful business.

Now we want to stop for a few secs, because the thought here is maybe you would like to see a little something. What follows is a very brief excerpt from the heart of a report of a Feng Shui master's visit to our tiny Republic:

General Summary of the First Floor Entry

The energy here represents the image of The Republic of Tea. It is peaceful, vibrant and growing energy. The lighting, plants and water features are excellent, providing Sheng Chi—vital positive Chi. The several placements of fresh flowers stimulate creativity. The aromatherapy candles bring fire-Chi to the area, creating energy. The decorous use of green color (wood element) represents longevity and peace. The bamboo is Yang and stimulates a sense of growth within the company . . .

Okay, enough for now. The main reason we stopped to slide this in is to ask some questions, most importantly this:

Still skeptical?

Shouldn't be.

Whether you realize it or not, you've experienced the endless flow of Feng Shui in action many times over. Do you know the feeling you have when you move the objects or furniture in your room until it feels just right to you?

Feng Shui.

Remember how your senses were energized when the house you bought or apartment you moved into felt truly right?

Again, Feng Shui.

How about the direction you face when it's beddy-bye time? Same feel-good comfy position each and every?

You guessed it, Feng Shui.

By following the basic principles of Feng Shui, you embrace the philosophy of synchronicity, that we are more than the sum of our parts, that everything has *Chi*. Your exterior and interior space, the sun, the moon, the stars, sounds, smells, materials, furniture placement, everything around you—all of it exists in harmony and unity with the terrain of your soul. This subtle yet tangible force flows all around you, through you, embedding you with mental energy, allowing you to free your real life and live it to its fullest potential.

Now, clearly, we don't know how any of this is washing over you, but what we do know is this:

To catch and live your dream, you must embark on a pilgrimage of clarity and personal growth, welcoming the practices, techniques and principles, that will awaken the sensory awareness which lies within and without you.

An ancient Japanese poem states: *When an old pond gets a new frog, it's a new pond.*

We urge you to experience a renewal, to journey beyond the boundless, where your unique possibilities come alive through the limitless enlightenment of a centered self who realizes the potential of its own true greatness. To feel the energy of the universe itself moving through your inner and outer reality, aligning body and mind, giving you the effulgent sense of personal power to completely and forever change a life.

Yours.

And how do we know this?

Because if you circle backwards to the beginning of the text, you know as we said earlier, that . . . shhhh. . . .

We've got secrets.

Secrets that we've shared with you these many pages, with the impassioned hope that you will share what you have learned with others who seek an inward light through a shadow of change.

So please, pass it on.

Because since forever, humans have been clocking time, pondering the existential mysteries of life. The same definitive question has plagued and riddled us throughout the centuries. The same cosmic quiz:

What is my purpose and why am I here?

Some spend a lifetime pursuing the answer to this

question, while others seem sadly content to accept the answers and consequences provided by their own inaction. Either way, it is a question that holds deep personal meaning and the most difficult of all answers.

Unless you are lucky enough to know the wonder and the truth—more precisely—The Secrets Of The Temple.

No need to engage the services of a Sherpa to deliver you to the roof of the world in search of an oracle of wisdom. We've come far enough together by now to know that by discovering your life's passion, by solving the riddle of your own potential, by dreaming the impossible possible, you begin to master the mysteries that can change your life forever.

Know beyond all question that you are a universal presence, a miraculous being endowed with gifts and with purpose that will allow you to become who you envision yourself to be. You have within you the actualizing power to define who and what you are. To become a Zentrepreneur and to evolve to your highest possible essence—to live the life you imagine. And if you ask the question *Why am I here?* we would be in wonder about what it is that you dream. And if you insist upon an answer, we would ask: Do you believe what you see, or do you see what you believe?

The absolute real truth of the matter is that The Secrets Of The Temple are, in point of fact, not so secret at all. The wisdom of the ages is simply and silently heard—a wordless anthem. Still, it is there to listen to in its pure and true voice, when you find the ultimate reality of what verily moves your head and heart deeply, beyond all else. So, again, if you were to force the question: *Why am I here?* what would we tell you? What would be the answer we would want you to grasp and have? Simply this:

Where should you be?

At least, we like to think that's the answer. No, we're sure that's the answer.

Yes, Regis . . . Final answer.

Day after day we live
on the edge of time.
Sun and Moon go as they may.
Opening and closing darkness.
Vitality, energy and spirit, forges
the glowing fire pervading great light.
A dream defined illumines Heaven and Earth.

ZHU MENG

Chapter Nine
AND IN THE END. . .

BORN
TO RUN

Wheresoever you go,

go with all your heart.

—*Confucius*

And so a book is born.

And with it, hopefully, a birth of wisdom that transcends paper and ink to shine the mind and light the way. As you travel the path, be guided by an inner wind, delighting in the garden you've been given and the glorious days that are certain to lie ahead. That said, please do us a favor here—as you go, leave a trail. Let us know from time to time how you're making out. Share with us your comments, thoughts and your happily-ever-after tales which have come from using the guidance and recommendations in this book. Reach us electronically at our e-mail address: **zentrepreneurs@republicoftea.com.**

And do come back to visit these pages should your shadow mind contrive a weakness of will or your spirit be in need of wings. This book was written so that you can read any of the ideas and perspectives put forward in or out of sequence, in the hope that you will continue to latch onto inspiration, attitudes and awareness that can help cultivate you, in your efforts to find happiness, harmony and true inner peace in your everyday life.

So, closing up shop now, will you please remember that yours is a life of limitless potential, that you were born to run just as far as your passion and gifts will take you. As Zentrepreneurs, cling to your heart and joy, liberating your natural energies, sending your life purpose graciously into the world, and be of no doubt that you will, as you must, catch and live your dream.

Until then . . .

ZHI HUI

Epilogue
THE RING
OF WISDOM

A book is like a garden

carried in the pocket.

—*Chinese Proverb*

We extend a moment of thanksgiving to you for having taken the time to read our book. That you have shows you appreciate the fundamental principle that you need to read to succeed. The surest way to become a Success @ Life is to empower yourself with the flashes of clarity when you expose yourself to new ideas and gain knowledge. We recommend that you assign yourself the noble task of reading one new book each and every week. You will find, as we have, that there is much to learn in this fast-changing world and that reading is a fit companion on your path of achievement. The more books you read, the better equipped you will be to take on the many challenges that arise from beginning to end. To receive a cup of tea, your cup must be empty. To receive true wisdom, your mind must be willing. Dedicate yourself to books that will help you make the practical life changes so you can Catch and Live Your Dream.

—*Ron Rubin*

For starters:

The Brand You 50: Or Fifty Ways to Transform Yourself from an "Employee" into a Brand That Shouts Distinction, Commitment, and Passion, Tom Peters

Direct from Dell: Strategies That Revolutionized an Industry, Michael Dell

Harvests of Joy: My Passion for Excellence; How the Good Life Became Great Business, Robert Mondavi

The Republic of Tea, Mel Ziegler, Patricia Ziegler, and Bill Rosenzweig

How to Become CEO: The Rules for Rising to the Top of Any Organization, Jeffrey J. Fox

Life Makeovers, Cheryl Richardson

The Great Game of Business, Jack Stack

EVEolution: The Eight Truths of Marketing to Women, Faith Popcorn and Lys Marigold

Zen and the Art of Making a Living: A Practical Guide to Creative Career Design, Laurence G. Boldt

Pushing the Envelope—All the Way to the Top, Harvey Mackay

Live Right 4 Your Type: The Individualized Prescription for Maximizing Health, Metabolism, and Vitality in Every Stage of Your Life, Dr. Peter J. D'Adamo

Feng Shui for Beginners: Successful Living by Design, Richard Webster

Rules for Revolutionaries, Guy Kawasaki

Sacred Hoops: Spiritual Lessons of a Hardwood Warrior, Phil Jackson

Staying Street Smart in the Internet Age: What Hasn't Changed About the Way We Do Business, Mark H. Mc-Cormack

Making a Life, Making a Living: Reclaiming Your Purpose and Passion in Business and in Life, Mark Albion

Do What You Are: Discover the Perfect Career for You Through the Secrets of Personality Type, Paul D. Tieger and Barbara Barron-Tieger

Doing Work You Love: Discovering Your Purpose and Realizing Your Dreams, Cheryl Gilman

Ben & Jerry's: The Inside Scoop: How Two Real Guys Built a Business with a Social Conscience and a Sense of Humor, Fred Lager

The 10-Second Internet Manager, Mark Breier

The 7 Habits of Highly Effective People, Stephen R. Covey

Peterman Rides Again: Adventures Continue with the Real "J. Peterman" Through Life and the Catalog of Business, John Peterman

Happiness Is a Serious Problem: A Human Nature Repair Manual, Dennis Prager

Running & Being: The Total Experience, Dr. George Sheehan

The Book of Five Rings, Miyamoto Musashi

The Harvard Entrepreneurs Club Guide to Starting Your Own Business, Poonam Sharma

Real Power: Business Lessons from the Tao Te Ching, James A. Autry and Stephen Mitchell

Growing a Business, Paul Hawken

Ten Things I Wish I'd Known Before I Went Out into the Real World, Maria Shriver

Leading the Revolution, Gary Hamel

The Tao of Pooh, Benjamin Hoff

Selling the Invisible: A Field Guide to Modern Marketing, Harry Beckwith

I Feel Great and You Will Too!: An Inspiring Journey of Success with Practical Tips on How to Score Big in Life, Pat Croce

Success Is a Choice: Ten Steps to Overachieving in Business and Life, Rick Pitino and Bill Reynolds

The Corporate Mystic: A Guidebook for Visionaries with Their Feet on the Ground, Guy Hendricks and Kate Ludeman

The Path: Creating Your Mission Statement for Work and for Life, Laurie Beth Jones

Journey to Center: Lessons in Unifying Body, Mind, and Spirit, Thomas F. Crum

Guts & Borrowed Money: Straight Talk for Starting and Growing Your Small Business, Tom S. Gillis

The Tao at Work: On Leading and Following, Stanley M. Herman

Tao Te Ching, Lao-Tzu

Zen Mind, Beginner's Mind, Shunryu Suzuki-Roshi

Who Moved My Cheese?: An Amazing Way to Deal with Change in Your Work and Life, Spencer Johnson, M.D.

Tuesdays With Morrie, Mitch Albom

What No One Ever Tells You About Starting Your Own Business: Real Life Start-Up Advice from 101 Successful Entrepreneurs, Jan Norman

The Rebel Rules: Daring to Be Yourself in Business, Chip Conley

Upstart Start-Ups!: How 34 Young Entrepreneurs Overcame Youth, Inexperience, and the Lack of Money to Create Thriving Businesses, Ron Lieber

The Anatomy of Buzz: How to Create Word-of-Mouth Marketing, Emanuel Rosen
The 12 Secrets of Highly Creative Women: A Portable Mentor, Gain McMeekin
The Measure of Our Success: A Letter to My Children and Yours, Marian Wright Edelman
Unleashing the Ideavirus, Seth Godin
The Art of Happiness: A Handbook for Living, Dalai Lama
Life Strategies: Doing What Works, Doing What Matters, Phillip C. McGraw

Acknowledgments

A trillion thanks to all the valuable and loyal Ministers, Ambassadors and Citizens of The Republic of Tea.

To the two mentors in my life, I am eternally grateful: my father Hyman A. Rubin and Julian B. Venezky. Their love and lessons fill me with pride and gratitude. Not a day goes by that I don't think of them.

To my mother, who taught me the importance of every day and every smile.

To Mike Patterson, for his wisdom of numbers and for his help in giving me the courage to take risks.

To Libby Griffin, who since forever has kept my business life in order and every day makes the impossible possible.

And, finally, to Stuart Gold, for his stand-by-me friendship, intellect and soul. His creativity, heart and commitment have helped me to catch and live my dream.

—Ron Rubin

To my parents, who encouraged me to dream the biggest dreams.

To my brothers Alan, Eliot and Ian and my sister Breana, who always continue to cheer.

To Albert and Jeffrey Fill, for being there at the beginning.

To all the wolves that raised me and taught me how to survive and thrive.

To our Minister of Design Gina Amador, whose talent inspires.

To our editor Allison McCabe, for sharing her keen eye and kind heart.

To Jane Wesman and Lori Ames, for their savvy, effulgent buzz.

To everyone at Newmarket Press and W.W. Norton & Company, especially Keith Hollaman, Harry Burton, William Rusin and Dosier Hammond, for keeping the roads clear.

To publisher extraordinaire Esther Margolis, for her insight and foresight, who a thousand years ago recognized a spark and urged me to put ink on paper and was there to open the door for me, still, all these years later, when I came knocking.

To Ron Rubin, my collaborator and my friend. His breathtaking brilliance about what's smart and important dazzles me every day. I am, and always will be, grateful for his invitation to breakfast and the opportunity he gave me to catch and live my dream.

—Stuart Avery Gold

About the Authors

RON RUBIN AND STUART AVERY GOLD are "Ministers" of *The Republic of Tea*, one of the most successful and fastest growing cachet brands in America today. Headquartered in Novato, California, *The Republic of Tea* sells the finest teas and herbs in the world to specialty food and select department stores, cafés and restaurants, and through its award-winning mail order catalog and website: **www.republicoftea.com**

RON RUBIN, the "Minister of Tea," is Chairman of the Board of *The Republic of Tea*. He keeps a permanent residence in Clayton, Missouri.

STUART AVERY GOLD, the "Minister of Travel," is COO and the lauded editorial "voice" for the company's Tea Revolution. He keeps a permanent residence in Boca Raton, Florida.